The Uneasy Conscience of a White Christian

The Uneasy Conscience of a White Christian

Making Racial Equity a Priority

Clifford Williams

WIPF & STOCK · Eugene, Oregon

THE UNEASY CONSCIENCE OF A WHITE CHRISTIAN
Making Racial Equity a Priority

Copyright © 2021 Clifford Williams. All rights reserved. Except for brief quotations in critical publications or reviews, no part of this book may be reproduced in any manner without prior written permission from the publisher. Write: Permissions, Wipf and Stock Publishers, 199 W. 8th Ave., Suite 3, Eugene, OR 97401.

Wipf & Stock
An Imprint of Wipf and Stock Publishers
199 W. 8th Ave., Suite 3
Eugene, OR 97401

www.wipfandstock.com

PAPERBACK ISBN: 978-1-6667-3078-4
HARDCOVER ISBN: 978-1-6667-2270-3
EBOOK ISBN: 978-1-6667-2271-0

11/30/21

Chapter 5, "Black and Wild, Like a Bear: Police Brutality and Moral Perception," was first published by *Faithfully Magazine* and can be read at https://faithfullymagazine.com/police-brutality-moral-perception/. Used by permission.

Chapter 9, "'But I Didn't Mean to Hurt You': Racial Microaggressions and Whiteness," was first published by *Faithfully Magazine* with the title, "Racial Microaggressions and Whiteness on Christian Campuses: Making the Invisible Visible," and can be read at https://faithfullymagazine.com/microaggressions-christian-colleges/. Used by permission.

All biblical quotations are taken from the New Revised Standard Version, copyright © 1989, Division of Christian Education of the National Council of Churches of Christ in the USA. Used by permission. All rights reserved.

Contents

Acknowledgements | vii
Introduction | ix
A Note on the Stories | xv

1 The Uneasy Conscience of a White Christian | 1

Joi: Code-Switching | 19

2 The Power and Effects of Racial Socialization | 23
3 The Harm of Whiteness to Oneself | 33

Beth: Forming an Identity | 40

4 Moral Imagination | 43

Jonathan: Police Encounters | 52

5 Black and Wild, Like a Bear: Police Brutality and Moral Perception | 56
6 Black Power, White Power | 63

Devlin: Systems | 75

7 Inhabiting Every Nook and Cranny of American Life | 79
8 Is Abortion Worse than Racism? | 92

Israel: Racial Undertones | 99

9 "But I Didn't Mean to Hurt You": Racial Microaggressions and Whiteness | 103

Ana: Being Latina in the United States | 119

10 Is Racial Equity a Conservative or a Liberal Concern? | 122

Lisa: Belonging | 130

11 The Resistance of Southern Whites to the 1961 Freedom Rides | 133
12 How Slavery Affects Us Now | 138

Jonathan: Church Encounters | 143

13 Why Church Integration May Never Happen | 147

Devlin: Breaking Down Walls | 157

14 What We Whites Must Do | 161

Endnotes | 165
Bibliography | 171

Acknowledgements

THANK YOU, ELIM SHANKO, for suggesting I write this book as we were talking in Blackberry Market, March, 2019, in Glen Ellyn, Illinois. You got me started. Thank you, Heather Donald Abraham, Shawn Bawulski, Sophie Clarke, Ann Eberhardt, Annie Michaelson, Sophie Miller, Alex Prus, Noah Ritche, and Hope Wood, for reading and commenting on one or more chapters. Thank you, Kendall Jones Stanley, for reading the entire book and giving feedback on it. Thank you, Craig Jones, for reading and commenting extensively on the whole book. I learned from each of you. Thank you, AJ and Kiki, for your contributions at the end of the introduction. I appreciate you. Thank you, Ana, Beth, Devlin, Israel, Joi, Jonathan, Lisa, and Sophie C., for your conversations that appear in the book. They moved me. Thank you to the twenty-five students and former students who contributed to chapter 9 on racial microaggressions. Thank you, Keenan Dava, for a conversation on the subject at Blackberry's; Heather Donald Abraham, for insightful email exchanges; and Hope Wood, for thoughts while we did a ten-mile hike through Herrick Lake Forest Preserve. Thank you to those who expressed enthusiasm and gave encouragement. I am grateful for knowing you. I am grateful, too, to the students in my Race and Justice classes at Wheaton College, who enthusiastically engaged with the subject. I also thank the editors of *Faithfully Magazine* at faithfullymagazine.com for permission to reprint chapters 5 and 9.

Introduction

WHENEVER A POLICE OFFICER unjustifiably kills a Black American, or when some other person acts in some clearly racially injurious way, one wants to ask, "What kind of person would do that?" What values do they have? What are their priorities? What character traits do they possess? The same questions can also be asked about those who actively oppose racially injurious actions. What kinds of people are they? What values do they hold dear? What are their priorities and character traits?

These questions run through this book. They presuppose the assertion that moral character affects the way we treat other people, in particular, the way we White people treat people of color.

This assertion strikes me as evident, because moral character plays an essential role in all of our interactions with others. Yet rarely is moral character discussed in treatments of race. News media typically do not carry stories about the character traits of people involved in racial incidents. It is the incidents themselves, the "objective" facts, that readers want to know about. Rarely is there a story about the themes behind the incidents—the hundred-year history leading up to the incidents, the sociological and psychological backdrop of them, the legal precedents that shaped them, or the character traits of the people involved in them. Though some books on race deal with the themes behind the incidents, they too seldom deal with the character traits of police officers who use excessive force or of activists who resist racial inequity.

Introduction

Moral character is important. Think, for instance, of the propensity to be morally imaginative. Those who have this trait to a high degree use their imagination in a variety of moral contexts. They imagine what it would be like to experience the pain that a friend is experiencing. They picture themselves loving someone in the way that that person needs to be loved. If they are White, they imagine what it would be like to be a person of color in a racialized culture. All of these instances of imagination affect how people act.

Think also of the moral perceptions one has. These are the ways one perceives people in moral situations. They too affect how people act. Those who are sensitive to the difficulties disabled people face will exert extra care in their presence. People who value compassion highly will be more likely to perceive that people are in need and thus will tend to act in compassionate ways. White people who perceive people of color as having equal value will tend to treat them equally.

Think, last, of organizations such as businesses, local town councils, or churches that take White authority and control for granted, that is, regard the authority and control of White people in business, town, and church affairs as "the way things are." The people in these organizations tend to look upon the concerns of people of color in their organizations as having less value than that of White folks, and they resist demands for shared power. The character trait here that needs to be eradicated can be dubbed "taking White authority and control for granted."

These instances of moral character in racial contexts point to the general truth that having the right moral character is important in racial contexts. The character traits that strike me as being important for those of us who are White are:

- Being sensitive to the experiences of people of color
- Being empathetic toward the trauma people of color have experienced
- Being willing to resist the tendency to feel superior to people of color
- Being willing to resist the propensity to exercise authority over people of color
- Being morally imaginative in racial contexts
- Having the right moral perceptions of people of color

Without these character traits, we White Americans would not be sensitive to the experiences people of color have. Racial equity would not be a priority for us, nor would we be openly welcoming to people of color.

Introduction

We would not understand why people of color are so upset when another prominent racial incident takes place. We would assume, most likely unconsciously, that being White is normal and that it justifies being entitled to certain advantages and positions of dominance.

It is no doubt true that we White people extend character traits analogous to these six toward other White people. But it does not automatically follow that we extend the character traits to people of color. In fact, as I try to show later, we White people who are otherwise gracious, loving, and kind do not uniformly extend the six character traits to people of color. Our assumptions about the normality and entitlement of being White are deeply entrenched in us. One of the aims of this book, then, is to show how we White people can live out these character traits toward people of color.

These character traits are, of course, desirable for all people. But it is not one-sided to focus on them for White folks, as I do, just as it would not be one-sided for a Black author to focus on them for Black folks. The traits are as important for Black people as they are for White people, though they are exemplified in different ways, given that Whites have dominated Blacks for centuries.

The character traits, in both their racial and nonracial applications, are rooted in biblical values. There is, first, the rock-bottom theme that runs through the entire Bible that all humans are made in the image of God. As such, all humans should be treated with equal regard, without unjust preferential treatment. Particular passages exhibit this biblical theme. The Samaritan who stopped to aid a Jewish traveler who had fallen prey to robbers on the road from Jerusalem to Jericho was sensitive to the experiences of someone different from him (Luke 10:30–37). He instinctively imagined how he would have felt if he himself had been beaten, stripped, and robbed. The Golden Rule, enunciated by Jesus in Matthew 7:12, enjoins us to treat other people in ways we ourselves would want to be treated. It does not limit that treatment only to those who are like us. Paul's great declaration of inclusion in Galatians 3:28 entails that we should be welcoming to those who are radically different from us: "There is no longer Jew or Greek, there is no longer slave or free, there is no longer male or female; for all of you are one in Christ Jesus." In both Paul's time and ours, these categories of people inhabit distinct social realities. Although Paul's declaration involves the law and grace he had been talking about in previous verses, it makes it imperative that we regard people who inhabit these distinct realities with equal respect.

Introduction

These biblical values, along with the character traits based on them, need to be taken more seriously in racial matters than they currently are among White Americans. This is a presupposition that runs through the chapters in this book.

Another presupposition is that we White folks must read and listen to the descriptions that Black Americans and other people of color give of their own experiences. This listening is necessary for the same reason that we must listen to our friends, acquaintances, and family members—to know how they have been harmed, what their feelings are, the standpoint from which they speak, and the contexts they inhabit. Without this knowledge, we will simply talk past them. We are not likely to have empathy for them or a sense of equity toward them. And we may become alienated from them.

This presupposition means that we White Americans cannot have well-founded thoughts about race relations in the United States without some knowledge of the horrors of slavery; White resistance to Reconstruction and the Civil Rights Movement; lynching; Jim Crow oppression; the Chinese Exclusion Act of 1882; racially motivated legal restrictions enacted by federal, state, and local governments in the US; Japanese internment camps during World War II; current ways in which people of color are treated differently; the damaging things that are sometimes said to them; and the tacit racial ethos in which we swim, often without knowing it. In particular, White Christians cannot have well-founded thoughts about race relations without coming to learn that the harm people of color have experienced in the ways just mentioned have often been at the hands of White Christians. The point of this reading and listening is for we White Americans to discover, from the standpoint of people of color, how they have been harmed, and to realize that this harm has been carried out by people just like us.

We White people must listen to people of color for another reason—to learn their perceptions of us White folks. Listening to the perceptions that people of color have of us White Americans is necessary because other people sometimes see our character traits better than we ourselves do. A therapist may recognize her clients' anxiety or anger better than they do, or someone may observe what is really going on with a close friend better than the friend herself.

This second reason for listening to other people is especially important in racial contexts. Drew Hart describes an occasion when he and a White suburban pastor were having tea one afternoon in a McDonald's.

Introduction

The pastor said, "I can't see what is printed on your side of this tea cup, and you can't see what is printed on my side of the cup," meaning that each would have to explain their racial experiences to the other. Hart graciously thanked the pastor for his sentiment, but responded that he, Hart, a Black college professor, actually did know a good deal about what was on the pastor's side of the cup. Throughout his life he had been exposed to history, literature, and politics from a White perspective. He had had numerous White teachers, watched television and read newspapers controlled by White people, and lived in mostly White suburban neighborhoods.[1] Hart was telling his White pastor friend that he could tell him some things about himself that he probably did not know.

Sometimes we humans get defensive when others point out truths about ourselves that we would rather not know, especially when they involve race. As George Yancy observes, "Marking whiteness in the presence of whites can be a profoundly disquieting experience for them, especially when the agent doing the marking is a person of color," which Yancy himself is.[2] Courage, however, requires that we not let that defensiveness be both our first and last response, but that we get beyond it to searching interrogation of ourselves. In this there is a third presupposition that runs through the chapters in this book—the need to listen to ourselves.

My Black friends decidedly and passionately concur with these three presuppositions. In a recent conversation, AJ declared that America does not like him. He has lived with this feeling for years. "I can't breathe," he stated, then repeated, with some agitation. A week earlier, Kiki described a conversation she had had with a White friend who had voted in a recent presidential election for a person whose policies would have had deleterious racial effects. "Don't you realize that your vote harms me?" she asked him incredulously. She has not given up hoping that her White friends who have beliefs that hurt people like her will change, but has redirected her energy toward empowering those who don't have the same political, economic, or social resources that White people have.

I want to be true to AJ and Kiki. To do that, I have to describe the character traits that are pertinent to valuing racial equity for them.

A Note on the Stories

THE TEN STORIES THAT are scattered throughout this book are edited transcriptions of interviews I conducted, most via Zoom. Joi, Devlin, and Jonathan are spouses of former students; Beth, Israel, and Lisa are former students; and Sophie and Ana are acquaintances. All are graduates of evangelical Christian colleges, and, except for Sophie, all are Black, Hispanic, or Asian Americans. I have identified them with their real names, which are used with their permission.

The stories depict in honest and raw detail some of the racialized experiences each person has had, beginning with a description of their first racial awareness. Except for Sophie, that occurred in their early childhoods. From there, the stories move in different directions. Joi explains the code-switching she had to engage in and what it felt like to break free from it. Beth tells how she gave up her childhood desire to erase her Asian identity. Jonathan describes in graphic detail several unsettling encounters with White police officers and later a number of incidents that deeply angered him. Devlin gives an account of how the educational system failed him, plus descriptions of what the church he is now a pastor of does to promote racial harmony. Israel describes the racial undertones in his early interactions with White friends, plus his reasons for feeling comfortable as an adult in different racial settings. Ana mentions several ways she must deal with being a Latina in a predominantly White country. Lisa tells how, off and on for decades, she has felt that she does not belong in White spaces. Sophie,

A Note on the Stories

who has inhabited White spaces from birth, describes the events during her year-long journey toward racial sensitivity while she was in college.

I was able to get these stories because each of the persons I asked knew me. Also, the occasion for asking about their racialized experiences was for a specific, public goal, namely, to appear in print in this book. It is not likely that Black, Hispanic, or Asian Americans would reveal what was said to me in these interviews in casual conversations of the kind one might have in a coffee shop or on one's front porch. Indeed, it is often better for White people not to ask people of color about their racialized experiences in everyday conversations, else their non-White friends be overwhelmed by the sheer quantity of times they would have to describe those experiences. However, as Lisa and Devlin mention, in public, church contexts, such conversations may be needed to maintain harmony and unity.

These stories connect intimately with the themes of the book in a number of ways:

1. Without a knowledge of the racialized experiences of Black, Hispanic, or Asian Americans, White Americans are less likely to be aware of their dominance.

2. By having an acquaintance of these racialized experiences, one is more likely to be persuaded of the importance of racial issues.

3. Knowing the racialized experiences of people of color can prompt White Americans to recognize their racial socialization, as described in chapter 2.

4. It is easier to exercise the imagination required by the Golden Rule when one is acquainted with the racialized experiences of non-White folks (see chapter 4).

5. Listening to the stories of people of color can prompt White police officers and other Americans to have the right moral perceptions of them (see chapter 5).

6. The stories supplement the statistics regarding racial disparities in the United States (see chapter 7).

7. The stories help one understand why the 1961 Freedom Riders did what they did (see chapter 11) and how slavery affects Black Americans now (see chapter 12).

A Note on the Stories

8. Knowing the stories can prompt churches to engage in interracial dialogue that may be needed to maintain church integration (see chapter 13).

9. Knowing the racialized experiences of people of color can prompt White Americans to pursue character traits that are pertinent to racial interaction (see chapter 14).

In general, the specific, detailed stories highlight the importance of listening to people of color, and they make the themes of the book come alive. They are fuel from which the flames of racial sensitivity can burst forth.

1

The Uneasy Conscience of a White Christian

I, A WHITE COLLEGE professor, had taught philosophy at Christian colleges for forty-five years before arriving at Wheaton College in 2013. Two years later, Wheaton, an evangelical Christian college in Illinois, changed its core requirements so that a single course could count for more than one category of required classes. "Ah!" I said to myself. "I will teach a course called Race and Justice for which students get credit for both the philosophy and the diversity in the United States categories."

Nothing, however, in what I had previously taught dealt directly with racial issues. Nor had I read anything about race, except for several slave narratives. I had, though, visited Black churches from time to time. And for some time I had regarded racial issues as important. So I was ripe for learning a good deal more about race.

I got the philosophy department's approval and the faculty curriculum committee's approval, then spent more than a year reading numerous books and articles on the subject. I read about the nature of race, the ethical underpinnings of racial equity, and Whiteness. I also watched a six-part television series on the history of African Americans, read more autobiographies, and read Frederick Douglass's famous Fourth of July speech, given in 1852.[3]

I never thought that the extensive reading I did for the course, plus actually teaching it a number of times, would change me. But it did, in numerous ways—ways that changed my conception of what it is like to be a person of color in the United States and ways involving my own self-conception.

Changed

(1) I became much more aware of the overt ways in which many American people of color have been discriminated against, including having fewer opportunities to buy houses in White neighborhoods, receiving disproportionately longer prison sentences, and being stopped by police officers more often. I had known a little about some of these, but had thought that most of them had occurred in the past. I discovered, though, that many kinds of differential treatment continue to exist, as shown by numerous statistics and individual reports. These include statistics showing that Black Americans die disproportionately as a result of encounters with police, that Black women die in childbirth at a much higher rate than do non-Black women for reasons that do not have a biological cause, and that residential segregation affects the quality of health care that Black Americans have access to. Other persons of color—Asian Americans, Hispanic Americans, and Native Americans—I discovered, also receive differential treatment, some in the same way that Black Americans do and some in different ways. The sheer extent of these differences was a jarring revelation. Each new bit of information I acquired jolted me a little more out of my "White slumber."

Knowing these facts meant that I would have to regard many of the persons of color I encountered as having been hurt in some way and to some degree by Whites. I could no longer believe that we had had the same experiences.

(2) I learned that the history of people of color in the United States has been ignored or distorted in history textbooks. This awareness began with a chance event on a Saturday afternoon four decades earlier. My wife had been on errands that Saturday afternoon and had randomly stopped at a garage sale, where she bought a book of slave narratives for a quarter. As I read the autobiographies of former slaves, I was stunned to learn that slaves were whipped and raped, that slave families were sometimes broken up when they were sold, and that they were prevented from learning to read and write—all by respectable and otherwise upright church people. My awareness of these facts was intensified by watching the six-part television series on the history of African Americans.

Nothing of what I learned from these sources had been taught in the White schools I grew up in. I felt betrayed by that fact. It felt to me that the true US history had been covered up. It did not matter whether that was intentional or unintentional. The effect was the same—ignorance of what really happened.

I was ignorant too, I discovered, of how Native Americans had been "given" reservations and their children forced into boarding schools designed to eradicate their culture, how Asian Americans had been constricted during World War II, and how Mexican Americans have experienced second-class citizenship in the United States. Although these people groups had not been enslaved, they had, I learned, been subordinated to White America.

Hitherto, my conception of US history was full of White heroes who founded a great nation with the noble pursuit of freedom—a cause of historical pride in me. I would have to set that aside and somehow integrate Black history into it—a history that is replete with White masters who denied freedom to the relatively recent ancestors of current Black Americans and who cared little for the good of those ancestors, except as pawns to produce wealth. I would have to integrate ways in which Native Americans, Chinese Americans, and Hispanic Americans have been treated into the White history I had been taught.

(3) I came to realize that I had thoughtlessly assimilated a sense of White normality, which, I learned, is part of the concept of Whiteness. I grew up in a little town that was totally White, and went to almost totally White schools, from grade school through graduate school. I lived in White neighborhoods, went to all-White churches, and had almost exclusively White friends and acquaintances. The authors of the books I read were nearly all White, and so were the visitors at the parks I went to. All politicians I had seen pictures of were White, the movies I watched had all-White actors, and nearly all the police officers I saw were White. My first teaching job was at a school that was just about all White. If there were any people of color in these places and venues, I did not notice them. Or if I did, they stood out as being different, as something unconventional and therefore anomalous. For me, White had been normal, the way people normally are, the thing to expect when I went someplace. Black and Brown had become other.

I did not consciously think of being White as normal. It had seeped into my mind unbidden and without my knowledge from the time I was young, as it did for a niece. When she was four she asked a Black friend of her parents who had been invited to supper why he had painted his face black. She evidently had only been around White people. White for her had become the standard way people are.

As a result of reading Black and Brown authors, I became aware of the fact that I too had thought of White as normal, even though I would have consciously disavowed that thought. After that awareness surfaced, I caught myself expecting that the bookstores and coffee shops I went to would have White employees, that the characters in the novels I read would be White, and that the composers of the hymns I sang in church were White.

(4) I learned from Black and Brown authors that this sense of normality came through to them as a sense of White superiority. Some of the White students in my Race and Justice class stated that they had initially resisted this component of the idea of Whiteness. This was not something that they wanted to believe about themselves. They were Christians at a Christian college who believe that all people are equal in God's eyes. But as the course proceeded some came to feel that they had, indeed, thoughtlessly assimilated the stance of White superiority when growing up in predominantly White contexts.

I also resisted this superiority component of the idea of Whiteness. Yet, when I thought about it with a vulnerable self-candor, I found that in some contexts I had felt that my kind of people were superior to their kind of people. This feeling was not directed to any individual person of color, so far as I could tell. Nor was it consciously chosen, but it was fused with the unbidden and subconscious sense of normality I had acquired.

It occurred to me that I had not picked up the sense of superiority only from the normality of being White, but also from the fact that I had had very few experiences of Black or Brown people being in positions of authority. And so I had simply assumed that White people are the ones most qualified for those positions.

(5) The sense of White normality, I found, had a deeper dimension: it was central to my self-conception. In contrast to the racialized conception of the identities of people of color, whom I thought of as essentially African American, Asian, Hispanic, or Native American, I had hitherto thought of my White identity as essentially what a normal, nonracialized human is. And this identity, I realized, was not peripheral to who I conceived myself to be, but at the very center.

In writing about "true integration," of Whites accepting Blacks as fully equal, James Baldwin states, in "My Dungeon Shook" in his *The Fire Next Time*, "The danger, in the minds of most white Americans, is the loss of their identity."4 Yes. If I were to give up the sense of White normality and superiority as essential to my identity, I would not know who I was. I would not know my station in society, my inherited place. I would be something of a stranger to myself. No longer could I savor pride in being superior. My self-esteem, based on that sense of superiority, would crumble.

One of the paramount truths about us humans is that we desperately want to feel ourselves better than others. We want to be on top, we crave admiration, we cannot live without experiencing some way in which we surpass other people. The insistent desire to be on top is displayed in what we do from early childhood to old age. It manifests itself when attempting to win contests, when seeking public acclaim, when getting promotions, and when regarding the racial group of which we are a part to be superior to other racial groups. Baldwin's point is that it would strike a blow at this desperate craving if White people were truly to accept equality with non-White people.

Another important truth about us humans is that this craving for superiority has snared us so strongly that we cannot easily extricate ourselves from it. It is as though we Whites are trapped in our White identities. Speaking of White Americans, Baldwin states, "They are, in effect, trapped in a history they do not understand."5 That history has been sanitized of nearly all references to White normality and White superiority. And, Baldwin hints, the sense of normality and superiority has blinded White Americans to the fact of this sanitization. The true history of the United States, I came to realize, includes events that were driven by a sense of White normality and superiority. But this fact had been obscured by that very sense. And this sense has had us Whites so strongly in its grip that we have been trapped in it.

With these thoughts in mind, I realized that my Whiteness has not just harmed others. It has also harmed me. Although in a sense my Whiteness was who I was, in another sense it was false. It was a social construction overlaid on who I essentially was—one who had been created by God to live with others who also had been created by God. In this respect, we were all equal, without racial hierarchies, without differences that made a difference in how we should treat each other. My Whiteness had obscured my God-created identity and with it the sense of God-created equality.

My sense of White superiority had also harmed me by standing as a barrier between me and God's love. How could I accept God's love for who I am if I think of myself as not needing that love because of my White superiority, even if that sense has been unconsciously absorbed? This haunting question nagged at me, and I wrestled with it.

(6) It also occurred to me that if I had thoughtlessly assimilated White normality and superiority, then other White people had as well, by the same sociological and psychological process of socialization in which the ethos of a culture seeps into its young, at least for those White people who had been in predominantly White surroundings. This sociological and psychological process, I realized, is common to all cultures. Prominent features of any culture or subculture become part of the way of thinking, feeling, and behaving in that people group. These features include values, unwritten expectations, class distinctions, gender roles, accepted behavior, forms of politeness, along with racial and color distinctions.

Knowing about American socialization into Whiteness meant that whenever I entered all-White or nearly all-White groups, whether for an hour or for a year, I would be surrounded by an undercurrent of White normality and superiority. I would contribute to this undercurrent simply by being present in the group. And being present in the group would reinforce my sense of normality and superiority.

I asked myself, "Can I remain part of an all-White church or other group, long-term, without having my sense of White normality thoughtlessly reinforced?" The only answer I could come up with was, "Not easily," though sometimes I thought I could fight the subtle reinforcement process.

I pictured people of color entering an all-White group—at a lecture, in a church, in a neighborhood—and feeling the Whiteness in it, feeling that the Whites in the group regard them as different, as other, feeling too that they have to be on their guard, and fearing that what they say will be judged differently because they are not part of the normal group. They would have felt these things for as long as they can remember. I suspected that my non-White friends would not feel welcome in the White churches I had attended, that is, fully affirmed and valued, not only overtly but implicitly as well.

(7) I read about institutional racism, but wondered at first what it means for institutions to be racist above and beyond the racism of individuals. I figured out that institutional racism consists of injurious practices and policies that individuals in institutions act in accordance with. Consider redlining, the practice of real estate agents steering Whites and Blacks to different sections of a city, thus causing segregation. It is individual agents who do the steering, but it is a policy that they are following. The result is

that statistics can be gathered to show that there has been disproportionate treatment. The same is true of statistics in health care, wages, and education. Though individuals engage in disproportionate treatment in these domains, they are not acting alone or on their own initiative. The business, school, medical practice, or church of which they are a part prompts them to act, so that in a way it is the corporate entity that is doing the acting.

There are numerous statistics about disproportionate treatment that various governmental and nongovernmental groups have gathered. Here are a few. In grade school and high school, Black children are three times more likely to be suspended than White children. In the court system, Black children are eighteen times more likely to be sentenced as adults than White children. A Black person who kills a White person is twice as likely to receive the death penalty as a White person who kills a Black person. In the workplace, a study found, people with Black-sounding names had to send out 50 percent more job applications than people with White-sounding names to get a call back. On the road, Black males are three times more likely to be searched at a traffic stop.6

The sheer quantity of these disparities makes it highly likely that implicit or explicit racism is involved in many of them, if not all of them. I found that I could not remotely maintain that racism is simply a matter of individual attitudes and actions. It is decidedly a social phenomenon as well.

(8) I learned too that the federal government, plus state and local governments, had explicitly adopted racially injurious policies and practices in the early to mid twentieth century. Among these were policies and practices that led to racially segregated housing across the United States. One instance of this involved the Federal Housing Administration (FHA), which in 1934 adopted a Whites-only requirement for insuring housing mortgages. Another was the legally sanctioned racially restrictive covenants in the deeds of houses. Still another was the location of federal interstate highways, which sometimes were designed to clear African Americans from areas adjacent to large city downtowns.7

I was stunned at the sheer magnitude of these laws and policies and at the effect they have had on the lives of people of color. Although I had been aware that the federal government had acted in racist ways in the nineteenth century, I had no inkling of official racism in the first half of the twentieth century.

(9) I learned that just because federal, state, and local governments later passed laws to make racially injurious practices illegal does not mean

that these practices have disappeared. In the first place, some of the laws have simply not been obeyed, as when some Southern states ignored *Brown v. Board of Education* in 1954 and violated the Voting Rights Act of 1965. In the second place, racially injurious practices not governed by law have still occurred, including implicit institutional racism and implicit individual racism. In the third place, there is still a social momentum that has perpetuated a racially damaging ethos—the laws made needed changes, to be sure, but there is still an underlying momentum that erupts from time to time.

(10) Among implicit individual practices, I learned, are racial "microaggressions"—"the brief and everyday slights, insults, indignities and denigrating messages sent to people of color by well-intentioned White people who are unaware of the hidden messages being communicated," to use the words of Columbia University psychologist Derald Wing Sue. These communications, he says, "are usually outside the level of conscious awareness of perpetrators."8 The intentions of those expressing microaggressions, that is, are far from the hateful attacks of overt racists, and yet the effects can be even more damaging.

I asked a number of students of color at two Christian colleges I had taught at about microaggressions. They gave me lists of things that had been said to them by White students. They also described how they have felt as a result of what had been said to them: shame, anger, resentment, inferiority, and exhaustion at the sheer quantity of damaging comments. (See chapter 9 for a full report of this.)

The microaggressions that White Christian students had directed at Christian students of color at these two colleges drove home, again, the realization that we White Christians are not immune from racist ways of thinking, feeling, and acting.

Altogether, these ten items made me realize that people of color have had very different life experiences from mine, so much so that it is as though we have been living in two different Americas.

These ten items also contributed to a growing sense of uneasiness, in several ways.

Uneasy

The first source of uneasiness stems from the fact that I have benefited from practices that have favored me because I am White. My good educational experiences, from grade school to graduate school, were had largely because

I am White. Without them I could not have become a college professor. My wife and I would not have had nearly as many choices about where to live if we had not been White. The same is true of the safety we have enjoyed, the good health care we have had, and the enjoyable places we have been to on vacation. These have all been due in large part to the fact that our being White has given us easy access to them. Nearly every segment of our lives has been shaped, directly and indirectly, by being White.

For decades I was totally unaware of these advantages. Now I have come to believe that they are, indeed, advantages derived to a large extent from my color, and, moreover, that they have been unjustly given to me.

I do not feel guilt for being the recipient of these unjust advantages, for I had no control over my being White or the system that has given advantages to Whites like me. I do feel guilt for being unaware of them for so long. I should have become aware sooner. I could easily have been on the lookout for articles and books that deal with race, and I could have thought more about the issues involved in race. But it is not this guilt that is a source of my uneasiness. It is the fact that the advantages I have enjoyed were acquired unjustly. I got them illegitimately.

An analogy illuminates the point. Suppose I had been given something that I later learned was stolen—"Oh, didn't you know that so and so stole some of those and gave them away?" I had enjoyed the gift—a ceramic bowl, perhaps, or a painting—but upon learning that it had been stolen my sentiment toward being given it would have changed. And I would no longer feel at ease in continuing to possess it.

It is the same with the advantages that have been conferred upon me as a result of being White. How can I have a clear conscience about having received them, knowing that the right to acquire good jobs, health care, housing, and education was stolen? I myself had not stolen that right, to be sure. But the system of which I have been a part has systematically done so, in varying degrees, and has presented me with advantages that depend on the denial of that right.

The uneasiness that results from this fact is compounded when I think of the further fact that I continue to be presented with these advantages and in all likelihood will continue to be presented with them for as long as I live. I do not have to worry about being stopped by a police officer for a rear tail light that the officer says is out or about how others will regard me when I enter a White space. I cannot evade these advantages, because the systems that I inhabit prioritize Whiteness.

The Uneasy Conscience of a White Christian

A second source of uneasiness is based on the fact that I am part of largely White groups and institutions—churches, neighborhoods, workplaces—that have systematically excluded people of color. Many Black people are wary of these White spaces. I have a Black acquaintance who once remarked that he cannot go into White spaces without tensing up. This is because he knows that he is not entirely welcome in those spaces. And I know that he knows this. As a result, I am uneasy.

Another way to get at this uneasiness is to ask why we White folks cannot set aside race when encountering people of color and see both ourselves and the other as simply human. The answer is that people of color have different histories, inhabit different spaces, and need different survival skills because of White normality and superiority. For me to abstract from these does them a grave injustice. It is also an evasion for me to say that I am going to connect to people of color as simply human. As Drew Hart puts it, "The common white Christian plea to just 'see people as people' is undermined by the highly racialized life of the average white person."[9] More specifically, Hart continues, "White Christians, especially, seem incapable of recognizing the contradictions of their utopian language and their distinctly and deeply racialized lifestyles and daily choices."[10] Simply seeing people as people is utopian, the ideal, the way we humans were meant by God to relate to each other. Hart is not criticizing that, as he believes in it. He is saying that White Christians who constantly stress the importance of this as a solution, as *the* solution, to racial bias seem incapable of recognizing that their lifestyles and daily choices are deeply racialized. Somehow, they are blind to that fact.

I am an average White person, and I have a highly racialized life. I cannot set that aside when I encounter a person of color. Nor can I simply say to myself, "We all are made in God's image, so we Whites should look past race when coming face to face, literally, with people of color." In the United States, these encounters are nearly always racialized.

The significant feature of this racialization is not just that there are different races. It is not simply that a person from one culture encounters a person from another culture. It is an encounter that is fraught with a backdrop of superiority and inferiority: the person of color knowing that the White person is part of a group that has viewed her as having less value, sometimes as being less than human, and the White person having been enculturated to believe that being White is normal, even superior.

Encounters between Whites and people of color are also fraught with a backdrop of White social power, "White capital." Those of us who are White have been in positions that enable us to influence others more easily than people of color can. We have had more economic and political influence. We have been in networks that enable us to acquire jobs more readily. My racialized life includes these ways of having social power.

I like to think that I personally have not done anything alienating to the individual persons of color I have encountered. I want to believe that we can be friends without letting the social superiority I have had impede that friendship. Still, "my" people have systematically excluded, subjugated, and alienated "their" people. And my people have done these to the individual persons of color I know, often with microaggressions and sometimes in larger ways. If we are driving somewhere together and we get pulled over, I am still White and they are not. And that is going to matter in how we experience what is happening. How can my conscience not be disturbed?

A third source of uneasiness comes from the fact that entrenched habits of thinking and feeling are difficult to change. Even if one's conscience says no to them, they can hang on, especially when they have been a central part of one's identity. They can pop up into one's consciousness, unbidden. They can surreptitiously affect one's stray attitudes. The Whiteness that has been embedded in me since I was a child may at times surface and undermine what I believe is a sincere and earnest commitment to a bias-free life. There is no quick fix to something that has covertly implanted itself in me over a lifetime. I cannot with a clear conscience say that I am absolutely free of racial bias.

I cannot say this, because I cannot say I am free of all sorts of troubling thoughts and desires. They inhabit my inner newsreels—those stretches of time between conscious moments, in which thoughts and desires flit about. They appear as I am falling asleep. They intrude into my mind when I am paying attention to something else. Some come from ways in which I have been socialized and some come from other sources. Among them are thoughts about race and Whiteness.

As a Christian, I consciously repudiate racial partiality. But as a socialized human, I know that it affects my thought life. This makes me uneasy.

The Uneasy Conscience of a White Christian

Some Responses

Lament

Though I cannot escape the racial uneasiness in me, I can respond to it in appropriate ways. One important response is to lament living in a severely racialized culture. Lament is the biblical idea of mourning for a painful condition. The psalms contain numerous laments, Jeremiah mourned for unrepentant Israel, and Jesus mourned for the people of Jerusalem, who had constantly rejected God's call for their lives. These laments are deep sorrows.

Such sorrow is appropriate not only for the racialized culture in which I live but for my own racialized self. I can lament having unknowingly absorbed the Whiteness into which I was born and having unjustly been given favorable opportunities that people of color have not had. I can also lament what I myself am responsible for—my long ignorance of the ways people of color must cope with White normality and domination, my failure to acknowledge my Whiteness, my succumbing to the temptation to enjoy my Whiteness.

This latter sorrow—directed toward what I am responsible for—is needed for repentance, which I should be constantly open to. It is also needed for apologies, which I may need to give to people of color whom I have offended. And it is needed truly to ask God for forgiveness for disregarding and disrespecting the value God has put into all humans. Because repentance, apology, and asking God for forgiveness are important Christian realities, lament is as well.

Listen

I told students in each section of the Race and Justice course I taught that the course would be an exercise in listening to people of color, because a high percentage of the authors that students were to read for the course are people of color. My preparation for teaching the class consisted largely of listening, not by asking individuals I knew what it was like to be Hispanic or Black or Asian or Native American in a White culture, but by reading.

There are numerous books and articles by Black and Brown authors that one can easily find on the Internet. In just the last two days I ran across an article on why Black Americans need to be in spaces without White people from time to time and an article on the psychological effects of code-switching. Both articles increased my understanding of the everyday survival strategies Black Americans must engage in.

This listening must go on for the rest of my life, because "the forces conditioning us into racist frameworks are always at play," as Robin DiAngelo writes in her *White Fragility*.[11]

Listening, though, needs to be done in a way that will increase understanding. María Lugones explains this kind of listening as "world traveling." "Traveling" to another's "world," she says, involves imagining what their experiences are like from their perspective.[12] It is for me to imagine what it feels like for a person of color to see a police car following them, what it feels like for them to be the recipient of racially motivated comments, what it is like for them to know that they have had inferior grade school and high school educational experiences.

This imagining, Lugones states, is a kind of perceiving. We perceive what it is like to be someone else. This perceiving, she writes, must be done lovingly and not arrogantly. This means that I must imagine another's world from a standpoint of equality, not a standpoint of superiority. I cannot genuinely listen to people of color when I perceive them through the lens of Whiteness. I must, therefore, set aside my White identity in order truly to understand the lives of people of color.

Set Aside White Identity

In one sense I cannot, and should not, set aside my White identity, because I will continue to carry that identity. I will continue to be seen as White both by those who are White and by those who are not White. I should recognize this reality for what it is—my living in a highly racialized culture. As I said earlier, it would be a grave injustice not to see myself as White and not to see a person of color as Black or Brown or as a mixture of colors.

In another sense, I should set aside my White identity as false to what I truly should be. Although I am tempted to regard people who occupy a lower social station as having less worth than me, such as the person who comes to my office to empty the wastebasket, I should regard myself as having the same worth. I should set aside that social station as irrelevant to true worth and exhibit welcoming acceptance to those who occupy a different social station. In the same way, I should set aside my White identity as irrelevant to my true worth and exhibit welcoming acceptance to all people of color in the same way I express welcoming acceptance to other Whites.

The Uneasy Conscience of a White Christian

This is hard for me to do. I instinctively want to think of myself as superior to others because of my place in society as a college professor and as White.

In an insightful observation, James Baldwin hints at a way for me to set aside my White identity. In "My Dungeon Shook," he declares, "If the word *integration* means anything, this is what it means, that we, with love, shall force our brothers to see themselves as they are, to cease fleeing from reality and to change it."[13] Based on the paragraph in which Baldwin makes this assertion, it is clear that he is talking about forcing White people to acknowledge their Whiteness. He is saying that until White people acknowledge their Whiteness, there will be no change in race relations. Until White people are free from the crippling power of their Whiteness, Black people will not be free from the oppressive racism that results from Whiteness—"We cannot be free until they are free."[14] What is most striking is that Baldwin is recommending that Black people love White people so that White people can shed their White identity.

Baldwin's assertion is remarkable for its insight into the psychology of self-identity. Baldwin states that Whites will not need to feel superior when they feel that they are loved. They will be freed from that need. They will be released from being trapped in a conception of history that is blind to the ways Whiteness has overpowered and crushed people of color.

Baldwin's statement can be given a religious twist. When we White people feel, genuinely and deeply, that we are loved and valued by God, we will not need Whiteness to shore up our sense of who we are. We will not need to think of ourselves as superior to people of color. We will not be afraid of the equality that is central to the idea of integration. We will be freed, liberated, emancipated to live next door to someone who is racially different from us. Accepting God's love casts out racial fear.

I do not want to be misunderstood about this point. I must continue to think of myself as being affected by Whiteness. My being born into a racialized culture, with its built-in socialization processes, ensures that. Yet I can regard myself as the person I was meant to be by the creator of humans. And I can do the same for people of color. They too have been socialized into a racialized system, one that attributes less value to them. So I must perceive them as having been socialized in that way. But I should also regard them as having the full value our common creator gave to them. I should not simply cast off my Whiteness, but should hold it alongside my sense of self as one human among all others of equal worth.

Holding these two sentiments alongside one another is slippery. One of them might overpower the other. My Whiteness might become so prominent in my self-understanding that it undercuts the sense of equal human worth. Or the prominence of the idea of equal human worth might obscure my Whiteness, as Drew Hart observed. So I must remind myself from time to time that both hold a rightful place in my self-conception, though in different ways.

Appreciate the Cultures and Accomplishments of Black and Brown People

In addition to individual superiority, Whiteness has typically included a sense of cultural superiority—my White culture has superior values and practices, and it has produced significant accomplishments, unlike Black and Brown cultures. I need to excise this cultural superiority from myself.

One good way to do this is to learn about the cultural practices and accomplishments of Black and Brown cultures and thereby come to appreciate their value. This appreciation can contribute to a robust sense of equality—my culture is not the only one that engages in meaningful artistic, musical, and literary undertakings.

This appreciation, though, does not mean that I should denigrate the value of accomplishments in my White culture. Indeed, I should not do so. For they too have value even though many of them have depended in some direct or indirect way on subjugation of people of color. It is not right to demonize the culture and accomplishments of Whites just because Whites have so horrifically subjugated people of color, nor, by the same principle, to valorize the culture and accomplishments of people of color just because they are people of color. I can regard the value and beauty of White accomplishments with the same mixed feelings that I need to have toward my self-identity, holding both the beauty and the subjugation alongside each other.

Have Hope

I can also hope for a day when color and race do not divide people in the way that they now do. Hope is not wishful thinking, but is based on a realistic assessment of outcomes. That assessment cannot be entirely negative, else it would be pessimism, and it cannot be entirely positive either, else it would be expectation, not hope. A realistic assessment reveals that people do change with respect to racial awareness. I have seen it happen. Others have reported such change. And there are countries that are not as highly racialized as the United States. A former student who is half Chinese and half Spanish reports that during the year she spent in a little town in Guatemala hardly anyone commented on her racial features. But her racial features have prompted numerous unwanted comments from people in the mainland US. (See "Annie's" comments in chapter 9 on racial microaggressions.)

Without hope, one might well feel like giving up. Having hope, though, energizes one to keep listening, learning, and changing.

Advocate

In addition to these general responses, there are specific responses I can have toward the particular ways in which I am uneasy. With respect to the first source of uneasiness—my unjust enrichment because of being White—there is obviously nothing I can do to undo it. But I can advocate for conditions in which everyone has an equal opportunity for enrichment—in education, job placement, housing, and neighborhood safety. I might even be able to be active in some of these. I can, in other words, use my advantages to try to dismantle the system that gave them to me. Doing this will not eliminate my uneasiness so long as the system remains, but it will put it into a context in which I do not simply passively continue to receive unjust enrichment.

Seek Associations

With respect to my White associations, I can actively seek associations with people of color, including friendships, business dealings, coworkers, and church people. This is more than declaring, "Hey! I have five friends who are not my color!" It is entering into the cultural spaces of people of color as a guest, with humility and willingness to learn and love. It is intentionally stepping outside the status quo of segregated spaces so that my sense of what is normal will change as a result of my associating with different kinds of people.

In some ways, seeking associations with people of color is hard to do, because there are not very many people of color in the contexts I am part of. Still, I can become aware of whether I associate with people of color as much as I do with White people when we are in the same context—work, church, neighborhood, or other assemblages. I can seize opportunities that I might otherwise have let go. And I can make an extra effort to enter spaces that people of color inhabit.

This individualized activity will not undo the institutional and systemic practices by which people of color are treated unjustly, and I should not think that having cross-racial associations is the most important way to bring about racial equity. For even if I succeed in getting a good number of quality cross-racial associations, the institutional and systemic practices will still exist. Those practices affect the lives of people of color in major ways. Changing them should be a top priority. At the same time, having cross-racial associations is better than not having them. They are simply good. And they can lead me to recognize that changing institutional and systemic practices is important.

This last point was made by the authors of *Divided by Faith: Evangelical Religion and the Problem of Race in America*. By conducting extensive surveys and interviews, they discovered that a high percentage of White evangelicals regarded individual cross-racial associations as the main way to deal with the "race problem." In contrast, a high percentage of Black Christians regarded institutional and systemic change as the most important way to deal with racial inequity. These differences flowed, the authors also discovered, from the largely individualized worldview of White evangelicals and the largely social worldview of Black Christians. In addition, they found that the small percentage of White evangelicals who sided with the worldview of Black Christians had a higher quantity of cross-racial associations.[15] Although the authors do not speculate about whether the associations affected the worldview, it may have been that this was so—the higher quantity of cross-racial associations helped Whites to see matters from the perspective of people of color. That is what I too must strive to do.

Retrain

With respect to the last source of uneasiness—the possibility that I will acquiesce to the White normativity and superiority into which I was socialized—I can retrain the habits of thinking and feeling that this socialization engendered in me. I can do this by consciously attending to the inherent worth of every person with whom I come into contact regardless of color, hair style, education, accomplishments, size, shape, manner of talking, or country of origin. This conscious attention can affect the unnoticed habits

The Uneasy Conscience of a White Christian

of thinking that sometimes have governed my internal reactions to people who differ from me in these ways. The habits may not disappear entirely, but their power over me can be considerably decreased by such attention.

I can also spend time in a context in which a person of color has more authority than I do, such as a church in which the minister is a person of color. The idea here is to undo the habit of seeing only my kind of people in positions of social power and authority. I must, of course, take in, or acquiesce, to the person's higher status in the same way that I acquiesce to the status of a White person in that same position. This too can go a long way in retraining my racialized habits of thinking and feeling.

Again, with Robin DiAngelo, I must commit to these responses as "what we need to be doing for the rest of our lives: engaging in ongoing self-awareness, continuing education, relationship building, and actual antiracist practice."[16]

None of these responses, though, will eliminate entirely the tension between what I am and what I ideally should be. The bottom line is that I must learn to live with racial tension. It need not, however, be crippling, and I do not need to wallow in the uneasiness that springs from the tension. Indeed, I should not wallow in it. That would be paralyzing. Nor should I regard the fact that I am honest about my racial tension as a badge of honor, showing how woke I am. That would be gratuitous pride. Plus it would be offensive to others, both White and non-White. I should treat my racial tension in the same way I treat other tensions with which I live—conviction and doubt, love and indifference, energy and indolence—namely, by striving to eliminate them while being aware of their reality.

Joi

Code-Switching

Joi was thirty-two when we talked. She lives in Arkansas, where she is a therapist.

WHEN I WAS IN prekindergarten, I went to a predominantly White Christian school. I was going by my first name then, which is Jennifer, and there were other Jennifers, none of whom looked like me. I thought, "I don't like my name, because it is not a Black name. It's a White name. The only people I know who have my name are White. I'm different from them. My name is not really my own."

Also, every morning we started our day with the song, "Jesus loves the little children, all the children of the world. Red and yellow, black and white, they are precious in his sight. Jesus loves the little children of the world." When I look back, this song feels racist to me, because it reduces people to their color. I did not like the song as I was growing up. I hated it. In prekindergarten, I'm sure I didn't know words like "racist," but I asked myself, "Am I really supposed to be here?"

As an adult thinking about this memory, it occurs to me that so much that happens in the Christian world, even in Christian education, is based on the majority culture. White supremacy infiltrates everything. The school's motives probably were in the right place—the White leadership wanted everyone to feel welcome at the school. But things could have been much better if that Christian school had done some research and thought a bit more mindfully about how we celebrate cultures that are different instead of simply ascribing a color to a culture. If I'm Black, I'm not just black. There's a culture to my skin color.

I grew up in a predominantly Black church that was part of a predominantly White denomination. We had lots of "the talk" in my Black church before we mixed with White people in the denomination. It had lots of gatherings, at headquarters, camp meetings, district events, and regional events. Anytime we grade school kids were going to be around White people at these gatherings, there was some type of conversation with us: "This is what we're going to do when we get there. This is how we're going to behave ourselves." The White people in the denomination had certain expectations about Black folks, so we had to be careful how we carried ourselves when we entered White spaces. This happened all through grade school. Even the adults in the church had to be careful so that they could protect themselves when they were in White circles.

Before I went to college, I had the same talk with very God-fearing, loving friends who wanted to make sure I was going to be safe when I went to a predominantly White institution. Don't be too loud. Be sure you speak clearly and articulate what you're saying. When you walk around campus, don't engage in too much loud behavior for majority culture, because you want to make sure that they feel safe with you.

During my sophomore year at college, two Black girls from church came to visit me. We stayed in my room the whole weekend, and we were really loud, listening to music, having fun. When they left, the students on my floor came to my room and said, "Joi, you were so loud this weekend, you were like a totally different person. We didn't know who you were and what was happening." I thought, "Oh! I can't believe I did that. I totally messed up." After that, I had only one of my friends come at a time, never as a group.

My future husband and I were in leadership groups at our college, and we got yelled at when we went on student leadership retreats, because all the Black students sat together at meals. We said, "All the White folks sit together too, and you don't yell at them. Go tell the White folks to sit with us at our table." But we were told that we were not celebrating diversity because we Black students were sitting together. To me, it was a White supremacist idea that something was wrong with Black folks congregating together when it was totally fine for White students to sit together at meal times. The same separation occurred in the dining hall on campus—either that or we Black students ate alone.

Joi

We wanted safety. If Black students were to split up and go be a minority at a majority White table, that would break up the safety that Black students had when they were together.

I felt safe with people who looked like me, who had a similar cultural upbringing, who had similar struggles. Maybe they knew what it was like not to have the lights on in their home. Or they knew what it was like to be working while going to go to school. It wasn't physical safety that I worried about—I never felt physically unsafe in White majority culture when I was in college. It was emotional safety that I needed, the emotional safety to be all of me.

The only time I felt that I could be all of me all the time was when I worked at a Christian camp in Missouri during the summer. The camp was led by Black people from top to bottom, and most of the counselors were Black. So I went from being a minority during the school year to being a majority and being looked up to by high school students who were from the inner city all over the United States. That camp gave me so much life. I finally felt safe. I could be all of me. I could be loud. I could scream and yell. Do chants. Jump up and down during worship. I could do whatever I wanted, because it was safe. No one was going to look at me like I was crazy.

Code-switching occurs when minority groups speak the language of the majority culture along with their own minority culture's language, and they feel the need to keep those separate. I have to be this way, and then I have to be that way. I can't be all of myself, my true self, when I am in a majority culture.

During my junior year, when I studied abroad, I engaged with all types of people and felt welcomed among them. When I became a senior, I felt emotionally safe enough to give up code-switching. I was done with it. I could not do it any more. I had to be who I am. And that has got to be enough for other people. If it's not, I am still okay. I'm going to be Black. That feeling of being truly safe is one of my favorite experiences from my college years.

It was a Christian college I went to. All of what I have described happened among Christians.

I still am not code-switching. That is probably the most freeing thing of all. I work as a therapist, and I pride myself on standing in my own shoes and being true to my values. This is who I am, this is what I believe, and I won't shrink back. That has only come about because of some amazing conversations I have had with Black women and African women from Nigeria who have shared with me their stories about what it means to live in their own shoes and in their own skin. I wanted that. It's available to me. God doesn't take away my ethnic identity just because I'm Christian.

So now I am grateful that when I enter White spaces, I am going to talk the way I talk, I'm going to have my own voice, I am not going to use a White voice. I am very proud of what God has given me, the skin that he has given me, and I want to honor God with all that I am.

2

The Power and Effects of Racial Socialization

When Linda and I married in 1965, there was no public talk of equal gender roles, at least none that we were aware of. So when we took up residence in our newly purchased mobile home, Linda did all the cooking, dishwashing, cleaning, laundry, and grocery shopping while I took out the trash once a week, despite the fact that she worked full-time. She and I had taken in the cultural gender roles that were prominent at the time without so much as a single discussion of household duties. We simply fell into the roles.

I am embarrassed to admit this. Our only defense, if it is a defense, is that we didn't know better. We were socialized into adopting these genderized tasks. They were in the air we breathed, in our families of origin, in our churches, in the culture at large. In different words, they were unwritten expectations, like the expectation that you not show up in formal wear or dirt-smudged jeans to an everyday supper at your friend's house. Your friend assumes that you know this. And you do, because it too is in the air you breathe. But in no place is it written down as official policy.

The unwritten expectations that surrounded Linda and me make it seem that the genderized tasks we took up were normal, almost necessary. Certainly the expectation about what to wear when you go to supper at your friend's house is necessary in some sense. You could not violate it without being thought rude or abnormal. You might not be invited back if you did violate it, and you might even lose your friend if the violation was severe and frequent enough. If Linda and I had encountered a married couple who equalized tasks, we would have thought them unusual.

Racial socialization into Whiteness operates in the same way gender norms operate. It too is unwritten. It seeps into us White Americans without our being aware that it is doing so. And the expectations it imbues in us seem normal, almost necessary.

These features of socialization into Whiteness give the socialization a high degree of power. They make us bond to Whiteness with the same strong attachment that infants and young children bond to their parents. We cannot break either attachment without disrupting something central to our identity. This bonding to Whiteness makes it difficult to become aware of Whiteness, difficult to undo it, and difficult to remain opposed to it once we disavow it.

Becoming aware of Whiteness may take a period of time in which we have occasional, half-aware glimpses of our Whiteness. This is because the bonding makes us fairly blind to our Whiteness. It does this because the Whiteness seems normal and natural to us. "How could things be different?" we think to ourselves, though this may be more an inchoate thought than a clearly defined one. The same was true for becoming aware of Linda's and my skewed gender norms. It took us nearly a decade, gradually, to recognize that they are unequal simply because they felt so natural. And it took time to make things equal. That started when Linda asked me to cook one night a week, and it progressed gradually over another decade. Undoing one's racial thought patterns also can take years.

Moreover, even if we Whites explicitly disavow our Whiteness, it will still pop up from time to time. We need to be constantly on our guard. The perfect story to illustrate this is the one that White Tim Wise tells about himself. He spent his life "fighting racism, speaking out against racism, researching and responding to racism, challenging racism in thought, action, and policy."[17] Yet once when he saw two Black pilots in the cockpit of a plane he was boarding, he instinctively thought, "Can these guys fly this plane?" Being the person he is, he immediately stifled the thought, beat it back, wrestled it to the ground of his conscious mind.[18]

Wise acknowledges that he had been conditioned "to see black people, or pretty much any persons of color, and immediately wonder if they're really qualified for the job—to automatically assume they aren't as good as a white person."[19] And this conditioning entered his subconscious mind, where it rose up on occasion into his conscious mind: "All it takes is a situation that calls forth the conditioning, the stereotype, that cues the response," he states.[20]

Some of the nonracial expectations that have been imbued in our subconscious minds are good, such as the expectation not to go into our neighbors' backyards or their front doors without their approval. And some are relatively unimportant, such as the expectation to keep one's front lawn neatly cut and trimmed. Some, though, are not good and have a strong moral importance. These include a class ethos in which we measure our worth by our social status and a racial ethos in which we measure our social worth by the color of our skin.

Another way to get at the power of racial socialization into Whiteness is to think of the fact that many Whites who have been socialized into Whiteness are otherwise good, gracious, and kind people. George Yancy pinpoints this idea with his discerning and haunting observation that "it is within the context of a loving white family structure that the vicious practices of White racism are communicated and learned."[21] In a loving family structure, one often grows up to be loving—empathetic and helpful when encountering people who suffer, generous with one's time and money, gracious to new acquaintances, and considerate of other people's space. Yet, Yancy states, one can take in hurtful attitudes and practices of White racism even though one acquires these loving character traits. One can exhibit these character traits toward other White people but not at all toward Black people—not empathetic or helpful toward them, nor generous, gracious, or considerate of them, or even mean, hateful, and cruel toward them.

How can this disconnect happen? It seems impossible to have such a divided character, even monstrous. And yet it happens, just because of the way racial socialization works: it influences us without our knowing that it does, and it makes Whiteness seem natural. Both the loving part of our character, into which we have also been socialized, and the racist part seem natural. So we do not see the disconnect in our own character. The result is that we are divided without knowing that we are. This dividedness is an effect of racial socialization, and it is a product of the power of socialization.

The distinction between explicit Whiteness and racism and implicit Whiteness and racism is crucial for understanding what racial socialization does. In his book *Look, a White!: Philosophical Essays on Whiteness*, Yancy states that overtly racist behavior is motivated by "self-consciously held prejudices, mean-spiritedness, and hatred," whereas implicit racial bias is a "pre-reflective" attitude that becomes a "structuring orientation" in a person.[22]

Although those who have the first kind of racism with its explicit racial bias also have racial bias as a structuring orientation, it is not the case that all those who have a prereflective racial orientation are explicitly hateful and mean-spirited in racial ways. One could explicitly disavow being racist in the latter sense yet harbor a prereflective and submerged racial orientation.

A "structuring orientation," for Yancy, is simply a feeling, attitude, or way of thinking that is a central part of one's character. These feelings, attitudes, or ways of thinking affect one's stance in a wide array of circumstances. That is, they determine the nature of one's orientation toward certain people. One might, for instance, be an untrusting person as an adult because one had been repeatedly betrayed by one's parents and siblings as a child. In the same way, one could come to have racially biased feelings, attitudes, or ways of thinking about people of color because one has absorbed the racially biased ethos of White America.

The significant truth here is that people bond to the values and ways of acting that they have absorbed as children. This means that these values and ways of acting feel normal and right. So when the racially biased ethos of White America is absorbed by White children, it feels normal and right to them. This absorbed ethos is prereflective because it is not consciously chosen and because it is a stance one takes toward people of color as a matter of course, without deliberation.

A key feature of this prereflective racially biased orientation is the sense that one is superior to people of color. George Yancy characterizes this superiority as the sense of racial dominance that has been bestowed on White Americans since birth. From it flows the sense of White power and privilege that is central to the Whiteness of White Americans.[23]

This sense of superiority was explicitly exhibited in slavery times by White slaveholders and has been since by those who have engaged in explicit, mean-spirited racial harm against people of color. But what about those White Americans now who disclaim any sense of superiority over people of color? Could they, through a "sincere act of introspection,"[24] declare that their conscience is clean, that is, they harbor no sense of racial superiority? Yancy is doubtful, because, he says, the "rabbit hole of whiteness" is deeper than White Americans suppose.[25] Its installment in White Americans via the absorption process while growing up has ensured that it cannot be easily discerned. It is nevertheless there, because of the near universal efficacy of that process.

The Power and Effects of Racial Socialization

What would it take to discover this sense of racial superiority? If one could set aside the "interest-laden and protective" shield surrounding one's deep self,[26] then one might be able to discern the sense of superiority buried within. Setting aside that protective shield is extraordinarily difficult, however. We humans do not like to think ill of ourselves. What is needed, often, is an "ambush" that strikes through that shield to our core orientation toward other people.[27] The story I mentioned in chapter 1 about Tim Wise encountering two Black pilots is a good example of just such an ambush. Another instance is a White person alone in an elevator tensing up or clutching their belongings more tightly when a dark Black person enters.[28] These surprise attacks can sometimes get through the thick veneer of good feelings we Whites have about ourselves to the sense of superiority we keep hidden from ourselves.

Several other effects of racial socialization exhibit its power over us:

(1) Racial socialization causes White Americans to "otherize" people of color, especially those with darker skin. This means that we Whites think of Black people and other dark people of color as markedly different from ourselves, as part of an entirely distinct class of creatures—"They are not like us." Of course, we Whites do the same with other White folks who are different from us in some way, such as educational level, occupation, accent, or political affiliation. But otherizing with respect to color is typically more extreme—White people who differ in certain physical features are typically not so otherized as dark-skinned people are from White people in general. Or so it is felt. And this feeling too has been imbued via racial socialization in the highly racialized culture of the United States.

(2) Racial socialization operates in institutions as well as in individuals, including businesses, governmental agencies, and churches. They too take in an ethos, which is perpetuated in the policies and practices of the institutions. There are complications with how this is done that need not be gone into here. The important point is that racial socialization has the same significant degree of power over the racial ethos, policies, and practices of institutions that it has over the attitudes and values of White individuals.

(3) Racial socialization also affects the way individuals assess facts about racial disparities, namely, with suspicion or outright disbelief. Suspicion about such facts causes people to ask about their reliability more often than when confronted with facts not dealing with race. It causes people to look for alternative explanations of the disparities. Both reliability and correct explanations of racial disparities are, of course, important. But they

are questioned more because of the racial socialization one has taken in. Or the disparities are simply dismissed as unimportant because they do not fit into the racial hierarchy one has inherited. One would like to think that established facts would be accepted by all. But predispositions to accept or reject facts are affected by the socialization one has been part of. Here too, racial socialization exhibits its power.

The implication of this last way in which racial socialization affects us is that because of it, the harm done to people of color is not as likely to be appreciated by those who have been socialized into Whiteness. An appreciation of this harm, though, is needed to have a robust sense of racial equity.

Appreciating the severity of the harm done to Black Americans and other people of color requires welcoming listening. Only with welcoming listening can I imagine what I would feel if I had the experiences of another person. In particular, it is needed to discover what I would feel if I were dark-skinned and had encounters with teachers who discouraged me from pursuing a professional career, or with people who constantly said demeaning things to me, or with a police officer who treated me badly. Without welcoming listening, the studies and stories I cite in chapter 7 and the microaggressions I list in chapter 9 will not persuade one of the severity of harm American people of color experience.

Appreciating the severity of this harm also requires breaking through the experiential world I inhabit to the experiential world of the other. Actually, welcoming listening is necessary to discover that there really is such a thing as different experiential worlds. It is needed to discover that the experiential worlds of Whites and dark-skinned folks are often starkly different.

Nikole Hannah-Jones, a Black journalist, points out this last fact in an article about why Black Americans often fear and distrust the police. "For those of you reading this who may not be black, or perhaps Latino," she writes, "this is my chance to tell you that a substantial portion of your fellow citizens in the United States of America have little expectation of being treated fairly by the law or receiving justice. It's possible this will come as a surprise to you. But to a very real extent, you have grown up in a different country than I have."[29]

It is difficult to comprehend this last declaration about inhabiting two different countries without a welcoming and open stance toward people who are different. Once Hannah-Jones's declaration is understood, though, the severity of harm that the racial socialization of White Americans inflicts on Black Americans and other people of color can be fully grasped.

The Power and Effects of Racial Socialization

And once it is grasped, one will be much more likely to regard that racial socialization as a serious moral harm.

Unfortunately, the willingness to engage in welcoming listening is itself undermined by racial socialization. The sheer power racial socialization has over us means that we cannot simply choose, out of the blue, to engage in welcoming listening. This is because choices typically are not made in a vacuum. They need to be preceded by relevant experiences and emotions that rouse people out of old character traits and move them toward acquiring new character traits. Given the highly racialized culture in the United States, we White Americans have the responsibility to seek out these experiences and emotions. We have the responsibility to be in process, on the way toward excising Whiteness and acquiring desirable character traits. Though Whiteness has been deeply embedded in us because of the power of racial socialization, it can slowly and surely be dealt with. It must, in fact, be slowly and surely dealt with for the rest of one's life just because of that power. The deep embeddedness of Whiteness requires lifetime work.

Sophie's Transformation

These themes are illustrated by the transformation of Sophie, a graduate of Wheaton College in Illinois. Her story may well be the story of other White people who had been unaware of their Whiteness but gradually became attentive to race. What follows is based on a recorded conversation I had with her shortly after she graduated from Wheaton College in 2019.

Sophie grew up in northern Virginia, just outside of Washington, DC. The DC area is diverse, but the spaces Sophie inhabited were all very White. Her church was White. Everyone she knew in private schools was White. The suburb she lived in was affluent and totally White. So Sophie didn't think about race at all.

During her sophomore year, Sophie was in a tight-knit dance and ministry group called Zoe's Feet. The people in the group were almost all White females. Anyone who was not White or female or who had not grown up taking expensive dance classes would have felt excluded from the group. It was completely monocultural. Everyone in the group had similar backgrounds. Sophie felt comfortable in it—the others understood her, and she understood them. No one pushed for any form of diversity. Sophie was never challenged to think differently, and she was happy with that. She felt sheltered and secure.

Sophie's junior year was a year of exploring. One of her new friends that year was in a campus group called Solidarity Cabinet. She had not heard of the group before her junior year, nor had she heard of the word "solidarity." The aim of the group was to increase awareness of the need for diversity on the college's campus. The meaning of "solidarity," she learned, is to stand with someone as an ally and advocate and listen to people's stories with a posture of humility.

Sophie's friend in the group was Asian-American. He listened to her as she began to process her racial identity. He let her ask questions that, Sophie later realized, were "pretty ignorant" and that probably were hurtful at times. But her friend was gracious with Sophie. Sophie also took a class on the rhetoric of civil rights that was taught by a Black professor. She went to his office a number of times and asked him numerous questions. He too listened graciously. By the end of Sophie's junior year, she felt completely convicted.

During the summer before her senior year, all the books she read, all the podcasts she listened to, all the churches she visited, and all the conversations she had revolved around inequity, specifically about race, but also about gender, physical disabilities, and LGBTQ rights—people who are in the margins. Sophie learned about social structures and her place in them.

When Sophie went back to Wheaton College for her senior year, she did a 180-degree turn. She left Zoe's Feet. That was extremely hard for her, because Zoe's Feet had been a community in which she had felt safe and comfortable. She could just relax in the Whiteness that had been a central part of her identity since early childhood, and she didn't have to challenge herself. But Sophie believed, as a Christian, that she has not been called to stay comfortable. She felt called to expand the kind of people she associated with. To do that, she needed to get into spaces she had never been in before.

Sophie decided she would visit the college's Office of Multicultural Development—the OMD, as it is called on the campus. It is a large room, much longer than it is wide, with a couple of tables for studying, a few random chairs, several couches, and a big aquarium. Besides serving as an office, it also functions as a hangout for students of color. It took Sophie a while to feel that she could step into it. She thought, "What right do I have, with my white skin and everything I represent, to go into this place, one of the only safe places on Wheaton's campus for students of color?" But her non-White friends invited her into the OMD, so she went.

The Power and Effects of Racial Socialization

Sophie spent a lot of time in the OMD studying and listening. Though she felt that her presence there was pretty quiet, she always had her ears up, because there were times when she felt that that space was not for her, times when it was a space just for people of color. She was very aware of her White body and her White privilege whenever she walked into that space.

The students of color in the OMD invited Sophie into conversations regarding race, from which she learned a great deal, especially the truth that firsthand experience is often the most valuable education. She even learned by taking an occasional nap on one of the couches. It took her a whole semester to feel that she belonged enough to do that.

In this way, Sophie entered a new community that she had earlier felt was not for her. Her friendships became more diverse with respect to color, background, nationality, ethnic heritage, and ideology. Her conversations expanded, and she encountered realities she had never encountered before in her "squeaky White spaces." Her moral imagination extended to the experiences of people who were very different from her, and she gained a sensitivity to those experiences.

Also, Sophie joined a group called Chalk Talk, a group of White students who acknowledged their White privilege and who discussed issues regarding racial inequity. The idea behind the group was to take the burden off the shoulders of people of color, who constantly have to deal with White people asking them questions about race.

Sophie continued to read about race during her senior year: a lot of James Baldwin, Bryan Stevenson's *Just Mercy: A Story of Justice and Redemption,* James Cone, womanist theology, liberation theology, plus books by White people who were wrestling with their White privilege—*Raising White Kids: Bringing Up Children in a Racially Unjust America* by Jennifer Harvey, and *White Awake: An Honest Look at What It Means to Be White* by Daniel Hill.

She listened to a lot of podcasts too, including one in the *New York Times'* "Still Processing" series in which two queer people of color talk about the intersectionality of race and sexuality, and one in "Inside the Pink" in which two Black women talk about their experiences as Black women.

Exposing herself to totally new worlds made Sophie uncomfortable. But she grew from that. She felt that she was in a completely different place during her senior year than she had been a year earlier.

As a result of all these experiences, Sophie now says that she cannot be for people, cannot be for the kingdom of God, cannot be for her sisters and brothers in Christ without being for the oppressed. The horizon of her desire to love others has expanded. She now believes that seeking to love Jesus means seeking racial justice.

3

The Harm of Whiteness to Oneself

NEARLY ALL TREATMENTS OF Whiteness focus on what Whiteness does to people of color. Rarely is what Whiteness does to White people themselves explained. This too needs to be described extensively, for it deforms the character of White people in significant ways. It consists of pride. It obstructs faith. It traps White people into a misplaced identity. It is addicting. And it produces indifference to racial injustice. Without detracting from the importance of the effects of Whiteness on people of color, I shall describe these ways Whiteness harms those who have it. The aim is to become aware of them so that one can root them out.

Racial Pride

The feature of Whiteness that is pertinent to all of the ways Whiteness affects White Americans is the sense of superiority White people have over people of color. We can call this for what it is: pride—thinking of oneself more highly than one ought to think, as Paul put it in Romans 12:3—with a racial focus.

If pride is thinking of oneself more highly than one ought to think, then it is also thinking of *others* less highly than we ought to think of them. That is, with pride we do not value others as much as we should. We do not regard them to be as good or as talented or as accomplished as we are, even though they may be. We regard ourselves as deserving more recognition, more praise, and more respect. Others' projects and activities are not worth as much attention as our projects and activities. Nor, with pride, do we regard others as having as much social value as we do. By "social value" I mean the ability to contribute to society in important ways. With pride, we regard others as having less value socially in this sense. At the extreme, racial pride causes one to think of members of another race as subhuman.

The opposite of racial pride is racial humility—not thinking of oneself more highly than one ought to think because of one's race. My white skin color is not what defines my being human. It is not what a normal human is. It does not confer on me any specialness. Nor does having black or brown skin color entail having less value as a human or make one less than normal. Racial humility is, therefore, an egalitarian attitude.

This egalitarian attitude is opposed to believing that one is more valuable as a human. To believe this latter is to be self-centered: "I am more valuable than those others who are less intelligent, less talented, disabled, or have black or brown skin." It is to "exalt" oneself (Matt 23:12) and "exaggerate" one's own importance (Rom 12:3, *Inclusive Bible*). To do this is to use comparison with other humans to inflate one's own sense of worth. This, in essence, is simply using others for one's own gain. It also makes oneself the criterion of the worth of others: "You are less valuable than I am because you are not like me." Both of these are an affront to God, because they violate God's measure of the worth of all humans. White racial pride replaces God's measure of worth with skin color as a measure of worth. God, however, requires that we not use others in this way, but that we respect them because they are intrinsically valuable.

When we have racial pride, therefore, we are violating the Christian belief that all are made in God's image and likeness. This belief is an equalizer—all humans have equal value. All deserve equal respect. No one is more special in this regard, and no one is less special in this regard. Racial pride, thus, is an offense both to other humans and to God.

Obstruction to Faith

One of the features of pride that makes it a sin is that it obstructs one's relationship to God. One with pride does not want to hear what God says about the need for salvation, or about God's ideal of human and racial equality. Pride says, "I know better than God."

The Harm of Whiteness to Oneself

With pride, one boasts, "I am better than other people, those who are not as capable or well placed or morally upright as me, and especially those inferior humans who have a different skin color." Faith, though, rests on freely given grace: "By grace you have been saved through faith, and this is not your own doing; it is the gift of God—not the result of works, so that no one may boast" (Eph 2:8–9). Faith does not rest on being better than others in any way. It requires a humility that is incompatible with boasting. Boasting undercuts humility, thus undercutting the faith.

One thinks here of the Pharisee and the tax collector (Luke 18:9–14). The Pharisee boasted that he was not like others—the greedy, crooked, and adulterous. He fasted twice a week and paid tithes on everything he earned. The tax collector simply said, "God, be merciful to me, a sinner." It was the tax collector's humility that made him right with God and the Pharisee's boasting that undercut that rightness. Racial pride operates in the same way. One cannot be right with God if one boasts that one is better than others.

Misplaced Identity

Racial pride undercuts faith in an additional way: it becomes an essential and central part of one's identity. Faith, though, to be genuine, must be essential and central. When racial pride is central, however, it usurps faith.

James Baldwin notices the centrality of racial pride in White Americans. To unpack this centrality, it is useful to repeat and expand his ideas regarding the identity of White people that I mentioned in chapter 1. In a remarkable passage dealing with the psychology of being White, Baldwin observes that White people "have had to believe for many years, and for innumerable reasons, that black men are inferior to white men."[30] Whites are "trapped in a history which they do not understand; and until they understand it, they cannot be released from it."[31] Baldwin is saying that White Americans have lived in a system that has caused them to conceive of themselves as superior to Black Americans. This conception constitutes a significant share of their identity, which is why, Baldwin says, White people are afraid of integration. "The danger, in the minds of most white Americans, is the loss of their identity."[32] This identity would be undermined with integration, because integration upsets the superiority-inferiority system of Whites and Blacks. Whites fear that if that superiority-inferiority system were to be undercut, they would no longer have a basis for regarding themselves as superior to Blacks.

The Uneasy Conscience of a White Christian

The nearly absolute attachment White Americans have had to this self-conception is illustrated by Baldwin with a fanciful picture. Imagine, he says, that you wake up some morning to find that there has been an "upheaval in the universe." The stars are all out during the day. They zigzag through the sky in random directions. The immovable regularity you have come to rely on has become chaotic. You would be frightened, perhaps even terrified. "Well," says Baldwin, "the black man has functioned in the white man's world as a fixed star, as an immovable pillar: and as he moves out of his place, heaven and earth are shaken to their foundations."[33]

Notice the strong words that Baldwin uses: "trapped," "upheaval," "immovable," and "shaken to their foundations." To say that White people are trapped in a self-conception is to say that they cannot get out of it. That self-conception is not able to be changed without an upheaval in how they conceive of themselves. If White people were to have that part of their identity excised, they would be shaken to their very core.

These strong words indicate that Baldwin is saying that superiority is an essential part of a White person's self-conception, not just a peripheral part. The sense of superiority could not be eliminated without severe trauma. The distress of doing so would be crippling. White people would not know who they are. They would have nothing to make them feel secure and safe.

If the sense of superiority over Black people were peripheral, it could be eliminated without severe trauma, perhaps even without any trauma at all. Imagine a novelist who likes to take woodland hikes from time to time. Her primary self-conception is "one who writes novels" and a marginal part of her identity is "one who likes to hike." If she were to acquire a disability that prevented her from hiking, she would be disappointed, to be sure, but she would not experience the same trauma she would have if she had to give up writing novels. Giving up the sense of superiority, Baldwin is saying, would cause not simply disappointment, but acute distress, because it is so central to the identity of White people.

Baldwin makes these points in a different way by asking why White people need n____s: "What white people need to do is try to find out in their own hearts why it was necessary to have a n____ in the first place, because I'm not a n____. I'm a man, but if you think I'm a n____, it means you need it." Baldwin then declares that it is the responsibility of White people to discover why they need to think of Black people as n____s: "If I'm not a n____ here and you invented him—you, the white people, invented him—then you've got to find out why."[34]

The Harm of Whiteness to Oneself

Baldwin is surely right. Being a n_____ is an overlay imposed on being Black. It has been imposed by White people because they have needed to impose it. And they have needed to imposed it because they have needed to feel superior to something. They have needed to feel this superiority as a central part of their identity, not simply as peripheral or incidental. This is true not only for those who lived when Baldwin spoke these words in 1963 and when he wrote "My Dungeon Shook" in 1962. White people in the United States are still socialized to believe that being White is normal. The normality and superiority of being White is so ingrained in most White people that for them the very idea of being human contains the idea of being White. Being White has become necessary to a White person's identity.

The centrality of racial pride in one's identity makes the possibility of its removal especially disturbing to White Americans, much more than if racial pride were merely a peripheral part of their identity. What if Black people were to obtain equality with White people? What if they could freely live next door to Whites? What if they could hold positions of authority over Whites? What if they could marry the children of White couples? These questions strike terror into the hearts of those for whom Whiteness is central to their identity. If the conditions they refer to became realities, Whites would have to give up their core identity.

The terror Whites feel at the prospect of having to give up their core identity as White explains the extreme reactions of Whites when their identity has been threatened—the Civil War, White resistance to emancipation in the 1860s, lynching for decades in the late nineteenth and early to mid twentieth centuries, fire hoses directed at Black children in Birmingham in 1963, violence in response to 1961 Freedom Riders, past and current police brutality, racist rhetoric of White US presidents, and much more. When Whites' "way of life" is endangered, and with it their very identity and sense of superiority over Blacks, only a strong and forceful response, they feel, would make them safe.

Though it is important to recognize these extreme effects of White racial pride on Black people, my concern here is with what racial pride does to those who have it. We now see that for most Whites, at least, it tends to become a central and necessary part of their identity, such that they would be terrorized if it were threatened. They completely and utterly need to feel themselves superior to Black people. This is, indeed, a severe harm to White people.

Addicting

Racial pride is not only central to Whites' identity; it is addicting as well. It is addicting because pride itself is addicting. We like to feel that we are better than others. We like the sense of heroism it gives us—we are the ones who should be admired by all. It is we who are special and unique. And because we like these features of pride, pride tempts. It lures. It makes us feel that we cannot live without it. It tends to hold us so tightly that we cannot easily loose ourselves from it. It becomes an obsession. We are fixated with it.

Pride is addicting because it gives us a sense of power over others. If there is anything that drives us humans, it is the passion for power. If being White confers this power, then being White will be firmly grasped. It will not be released without extreme upheaval.

Feeling pride can easily become habitual, which is to say that it can easily become an addiction. It can control us so that our automatic response in relevant circumstances is to be proud. When this is the case, those of us who are White automatically respond with racial pride whenever we encounter a person of color.

It is a general truth that neither individuals nor institutions change easily, and this truth is especially operative when it comes to protecting a sense of racial superiority. It is nearly intractable.

Produces Faulty Moral Perceptions and Indifference

Having a sense of superiority over Black people produces faulty moral perceptions. This is because a sense of superiority distorts one's perception of the true value of Black people. It makes one think that Black people have less value than they actually do. When this happens, one's instinctive moral perceptions of Black people will be skewed.

A number of conditions can distort moral perceptions. Being part of a particular social group is one of them. To be White in the United States is to be part of a social group, not a cohesive one, to be sure, but nevertheless a group. As such, its members typically have an in-group–out-group mindset to some degree—those in my group, the ones who are like me, are more readily perceived to be acceptable and good, whereas those outside my group, the ones who are not like me, are less readily perceived to be acceptable and good. When a sense of superiority is added to this phenomenon, I become more likely to perceive those outside my group as inferior.

When I do that, I tend to be indifferent to the plight of people who are not in my group. I am less likely to have concern for harms done to them or for their safety, health, education, housing, and job opportunities. I am likely not to have compassion or a sense of fairness. To have these, I must cast out pride. Otherwise, I will remain unconcerned about and detached from the experiences of Black Americans. I will be indifferent to the inferior conditions in which they often live and the racial disparities they commonly experience.

Operates Implicitly

It is important to say that these harms nearly always exist in the same way that implicit racism exists, namely, behind the scenes, without being explicitly conscious to the one who is harmed. Except for Ku Klux Klan–type people, White people do not consciously boast, "I value myself more than you" or "My race is superior to your race." Most White people's sense of being part of a superior race lies below full awareness to some degree. So does their misplaced identity in Whiteness. Whiteness does not explicitly acknowledge that being White is central to one's identity. Nor is one aware that one is addicted to that identity. One can, in short, be harmed without being aware of it.

Beth

Forming an Identity

Beth is currently in her fourth year of medical school in New York City.

MY BIRTH MOTHER IS Chinese, and my birth father is Korean, so I am half-Chinese and half-Korean by birth. But my adoptive parents are both Chinese, so I identify a lot more with Chinese culture.

My first instance of racial awareness happened quite early, because my adopted younger sister is Black, and my parents were intentional about having conversations about ethnicity and, by extrapolation, race. Also, we were treated differently. When we ate at Chinese restaurants, I always got chopsticks and a little cup of hot tea, while my sister always got a metal fork and a glass of ice water. Or people spoke to me in Chinese because they assumed that I speak Chinese, which I don't.

In school, there were spoken and unspoken assumptions that I was better at academics than my sister, and people were surprised when she did well but nodded understandingly if she didn't. When she and I walked around our neighborhood, which is quite upper class, those who walked by us looked back because they were not used to someone who looks like my sister in our neighborhood. She now has children, and when we are out together people assume that she's my nanny. They address me as a mother, thinking that my sister is hired to look after my children. This is quite uncomfortable for me and her.

Beth

The California city we grew up in is very White and very Asian, so as a child I did not feel like a minority in terms of numbers. However, I was still the recipient of racialized comments that made me not want to be Asian. There were the classic schoolyard moments—pulling the corners of eyes into a slant, asking whether I ate dogs—plus disparaging comments about the food my mom packed for lunch. I wanted to bring Lunchables to school because all my White classmates had Lunchables. But my mom made me sushi rolls and fried rice. I was embarrassed by that. My classmates said things like, "Your food smells weird."

When I was five or six, I wanted to change the way I looked so badly that I ate tons and tons of blueberries because I thought that if I ate enough my eyes would turn blue. I wanted to have blond hair like my White classmates. I wished that my face looked different. I wanted a double eyelid. I wore clothes and used certain words that made me appear more Caucasian, to the point that people said, "You're whitewashed, like a banana—yellow on the outside but really a white person." That made me so happy when I was in middle and high school. The goal was to erase my Asian identity.

I can't pinpoint a particular time when this changed, though taking the Race and Justice class at Wheaton College played a large part in embracing my Asian identity. I was excited during class discussions to hear what Black, Hispanic, and other classmates of color had to offer to the discussions. That made me think, "If I'm excited about the perspectives that they are bringing to our conversations, why do I not feel excited about the perspective I can bring to a conversation?" This was the first time I had listened to other people of color share their experiences, and it was the first time I realized that I too had experiences to share.

White students in the class wanted to hear what we people of color had to say. Up until then, I had not thought that White people were interested in me as an Asian person. When I heard them listening to us people of color, it made me realize that if other people value my perspective as a person of color, I need to respect myself as a person of color.

It is a little ironic that I needed to hear that my voice was valued by White people before I felt comfortable stepping into my identity as an Asian. My adoptive parents, who are immigrants from Hong Kong, thought a great deal about how to fit into White spaces in the United States. And I spent so much of my life thinking of how to assimilate seamlessly into these spaces that it never occurred to me to change the spaces by bringing my unique perspective into them. It was a big moment for me when I realized

The Uneasy Conscience of a White Christian

I could do this. I discovered that I had a unique perspective that could enrich the White spaces I was in, instead of trying to conform myself to the people in those spaces. And so I embraced my heritage and my identity as a blended daughter of Chinese American immigrants.

Lately, I have been wondering how I can speak into the tensions that exist between the White and Black communities. How can I partner with other communities of color and be an advocate for them? This is a poignant question because historically Asian Americans have had a lot of anti-Black racism. It is also a very pertinent question to me because of recent anti-Asian hate crimes. I have never experienced what my sister and other Black people have experienced. I have never felt myself in danger. But now it feels different. I feel trepidation at being an outsider in my own city. The idea of being targeted as I walk around the Bronx or Manhattan because of how I look by someone who doesn't know anything about me is very unsettling. I feel vulnerable. And so I have been thinking a lot about the fact that my sister and my Black friends have been living with these feelings for their whole lives. For them, that is a normal part of life. I can now appreciate the underlying fear of being colored in America.

For a long time, the Asian American community, including me, has assumed that if we try hard enough to assimilate to White American culture, we will be accepted, and with that will come privileges. But the recent rise in anti-Asian violence lifts the cover on that assumption. It reveals that no matter how hard we try, we will always be perceived as other. I think that is almost as unsettling to us Asian Americans as the actual violence itself.

A decent portion of the Asian community in the United States has bought into the model minority myth—if we keep our heads down, work super hard, and don't make too much of a fuss, we can be peacefully accepted into the White American system and achieve the dreams we set out to achieve when we moved to this country. But now I think that current anti-Asian events are casting doubt on that assumption. Now I wonder whether dispelling the model minority myth, instead of trying to live into it, would be helpful to the Asian community.

4

Moral Imagination

I ONCE ASKED A class I was teaching whether anyone had ever heard a sermon on moral imagination. One person raised her hand. Like the rest of the class, I had not, though I had heard a small part of a sermon years earlier that dealt with imagination. Much more needs to be said about it, though, because it is needed for empathy, rightly applying the Golden Rule, and a sense of racial fairness.

Empathy, the Golden Rule, and Racial Fairness

To have empathy, one must be aware of, and sensitive to, the feelings, thoughts, and experiences of another. Usually these feelings, thoughts, and experiences are painful, but they can also be happy. One can, for example, empathize with the happy delight of a new mother or with the elation of one who is newly engaged. When we do, we are likely to feel a similar delight and elation, along with a desire to express those feelings to the one with whom we empathize. It is the same when we empathize with the grief of one whose spouse has died or the anger of one who has been unjustifiably harmed. Here too, we are likely to feel a vicarious grief and anger and want to express them to the one with whom we empathize. Empathy is at play both when we "rejoice with those who rejoice" and when we "weep with those who weep" (Rom 12:15).

Notice that it is possible to observe someone experiencing delight or sorrow without feeling empathy toward them. The simple knowledge that another is having an emotion is not enough to have empathy. There must, in addition, be a sensitivity to the value of the emotion to the one who has it—a regard for the importance of the delight and sorrow to those who experience these. I might, for instance, know that people are starving in poor countries but feel no empathy for them, or know that my next-door neighbor has become unemployed but have no empathy for the neighbor. To have empathy, I must regard the painful experiences in each case as important to those who have them. And to have this regard, I must exercise imagination.

I must imagine what it is like for someone to become a new mother or to be unjustifiably harmed. I do not need to have been a mother or unjustifiably harmed to imagine these, though I do need to have a reservoir of experiences on which I can base my imagining. The larger this reservoir is, the more readily I will be able to imagine what other people experience. I might never have had a stranger touch my hair out of curiosity, but I have had other intrusive experiences, and thereby can imagine what my Black acquaintances feel when someone touches their hair just to feel what it is like. In particular, I have on occasion felt resentment when someone has violated my expectations of personal propriety. So I can feel the resentment of people of color when they tell me about violations of their personal space. And I can feel the importance that they attach to that resentment, because I have had resentment in different contexts to which I attached importance. I do not, of course, actually have their resentment—only they can have their own feelings. But I do imagine them having a feeling like the one that I have had.

In a similar way, imagination is needed to apply the Golden Rule: do to others as you would have them do to you (the positive version), and do not do to others what you would not have them do to you (the negative version). The unstated assumption in the Golden Rule can be expressed in a reformulation of it: do to others as you would have them do to you *if you were in their condition*. If I were on crutches because of a broken ankle, I would want someone to open a door for me when entering a building. And I would not want people bumping into me, which means that I would want them to exercise care when near me. If I were a person of color, I would want to be treated with the same care and respect with which others are treated. I would not want to be unjustifiably discriminated against.

Moral Imagination

Applying the Golden Rule requires that we picture ourselves being in the condition other people are in. Those of us who are not on crutches must picture ourselves being on crutches and then imagine how we would and would not want to be treated because of being on crutches. Similarly, those of us who are White must picture ourselves being a person of color and then imagine how we would and would not want to be treated because of being a person of color. We would not want to be turned away from a job or a scholarship just because of our skin color. So, the Golden Rule says, members of the dominant race must not turn away others just because of they are of a different race.

Last, imagination is needed to have a sense of racial fairness, because a sense of racial fairness is dependent on empathy and rightly applying the Golden Rule. I need empathy to sense that racial fairness is an important value, because without empathy I will not feel the importance of a person of color's pain when being discriminated against. The more that I feel that pain, the more I will become convinced of the need for racial fairness. And the better I am able to imagine someone experiencing that pain, the better I will be able to empathize with them.

It is the same with the Golden Rule. When I apply it rightly, I will picture myself being Black or Brown or Asian. I will imagine that I might not be welcomed by my new neighbors when I move to a new house or that someone might use a hurtful stereotype when saying something to me. I would not like be treated this way, I realize, when I perform this act of imagination. I conclude that I should welcome new neighbors who are people of color just as much as I would welcome new neighbors who are not people of color. I should be vigilant to avoid saying things that are based on hurtful stereotypes about people of color. By using imagination when applying the Golden Rule in racial contexts, I can, again, become convinced of the importance of racial fairness.

The power of moral imagination, which is simply the use of imagination in moral contexts, can be illustrated with a couple of examples. Richard Rothstein, in his *The Color of Law: A Forgotten History of How Our Government Segregated America*, explains how asthma affects the educational achievement of low-income African American children who live in segregated areas. Such children suffer from asthma "at nearly twice the rate of white children—probably because African Americans live in or near residential-industrial neighborhoods with more dust, pollutants, and vermin. Asthmatic children are more likely to awaken at night wheezing and, if they come to school after an episode, can be drowsy and less able to pay attention."[35] Because of this, Rothstein concludes, "high average achievement is almost impossible to realize in a low-income, segregated school, embedded in a segregated neighborhood." Lead poisoning contributes to this inability: "African American children have dangerous and irreversible lead-in-blood levels at twice the rate of white children." When lead gets into the brains of young children, they are less able to exercise self-control. To be sure, Rothstein says, some children overcome these conditions and perform at higher-than-average levels. But, on average, "a student with problems like these, stemming from life in segregated neighborhoods, performs more poorly."[36]

An empathetic person, one who has a tendency to respond with empathy to facts such as these, will instinctively imagine herself being an African American child who lives in a segregated neighborhood and who is afflicted with asthma. She will picture herself having less energy to absorb what her teachers are saying in class and less energy to do homework. She will imagine what her life chances are because of not being able to do as well in school because she has less energy. This will prompt her to picture the larger context in which she, as an asthmatic child, lives. She will realize that there are social forces that have made it likely that she has asthma, which later will cause her to have fewer opportunities to make something of herself.

The person who imagines herself being an asthmatic African American child will imagine that she would almost certainly feel resentment that these social forces exist. She will want there to be other social forces that even things out, that is, make it such that African American children are no more likely to get asthma than White children do. In this way, the imagination that is employed in empathy and the Golden Rule will lead to the conviction that social forces must change for there to be racial fairness. All of this is true for lead poisoning as well, or anything else in segregated or family life that contributes to a child's lower educational achievement.

Consider too reports of excessive use of force by police when dealing with Black Americans. An empathetic person will immediately imagine what recipients of this force feel. She will also imagine what other Black Americans feel about those reports and will know, as a result of this second imaginative act, that other Black Americans will fear encounters with White police officers even though they themselves have not had such an encounter. This empathy will lead the person to want police officers to change the way they behave toward people who are different from them, perhaps with official training programs. In this case too, the desire for racial fairness springs from empathy.

Obstacles

Both Whiteness and self-centeredness can block moral imagination. The two elements of Whiteness that are pertinent to this blockage are the normality and the superiority of being White. When someone thinks of being White as normal, one typically thinks of being Black as abnormal, perhaps even alien or subhuman. To ask a White person with this conception of being Black to imagine that they are Black would instantly provoke resistance. This resistance would make a White person literally unable to conceive of themselves being Black. The same is true of someone who thinks of being White as superior to being Black. Superiority is a moral concept—"we Whites have more worth than you Blacks." This sense too prevents a White person from imagining herself being Black.

In addition to the racial self-centeredness of Whiteness, general self-centeredness blocks moral imagination. When one is constantly preoccupied with oneself, one cannot easily be other-directed, which is required to imagine the pain or pleasure that another experiences. The moral effort of focusing on another's experience is often too much for one whose attention is largely self-directed.

These points about what can block moral imagination were driven home one day in my Race and Justice class. I had raised the question of how a 1950s Southern White sheriff such as Clarence Strider, who in 1955 in Tallahatchie County, Mississippi, was involved in the Emmett Till case, could have been persuaded to give up his racism. We needed a real, live sheriff to answer that question, I said. Alex shot his hand up. He would pretend to be a Southern White sheriff and the rest of the class would try to convince him to change. Here is a snippet of the ensuing dialogue:

> **Class member**: Do you think of Black people as fellow human beings who deserve equal respect, or not?
>
> **White sheriff**: Blacks are different from we White people, and equal respect is not part of the equation.
>
> **Class member**: Don't you believe that everyone should be treated equally?

White sheriff: I believe that the races should be separate. Blacks and Whites should not intermingle.

Class member: How would you feel if you were Black and someone discriminated against you because of it?

White sheriff: I am not Black, so there is no point in asking what I would feel if I were.

Class member: What about disparities in education and health care between White Americans and Black Americans?

White sheriff: I am not responsible for how Blacks live.

Class member: Mr. Sheriff, I want you to imagine that you are Black so you can feel what they are experiencing when we White people treat them differently. Can you do that?

White sheriff: That question is totally irrelevant. Why are you asking it? You sound like some liberal or communist who wants to prove something. What is your agenda?

After ten minutes, the class gave up. Alex, with some help from me, had proven to be intractable. Moral imagination, empathy, and racial fairness were totally foreign to him, and the class could not get him to see their importance. He remained a confirmed racist. The real Alex was somewhat shaken by the answers he had given to the class as an imaginary racist. How, he asked, with visible agony, could you ever convince someone who is so set in their ways to have empathy for people who are different from them? How could you get them to imagine the effects of their racism on Black people?

These are haunting questions. One is tempted to retreat from them with resignation—some people just cannot change, or will not change. Try as we might, we cannot do anything to get them to have racial empathy. They remain entrenched in their racial shell, which nothing can puncture.

This, apparently, is what happened to Bull Connor, one of the most well-known Southern White sheriffs. In 1963, as Commissioner of Public Safety in Birmingham, he ordered police officers and firefighters to use dogs and high-pressure water hoses against demonstrators, an event that brought national attention to the Civil Rights Movement. He died in 1973. His biographer wrote, "Unlike some white supremacist leaders of his time, Connor was unrepentant and never repudiated his defense of racial segregation."[37]

Moral Imagination

Nurturing Moral Imagination

Perhaps the thing to do, instead of admitting defeat, is to answer a different question: How can I nurture moral imagination in myself? After all, I am not perfectly free from either racial or general self-centeredness. Even though I exercise moral imagination in a number of ways, there may be further arenas in which I am more like the 1950s Southern White sheriff than I realize. And perhaps, too, answering the question about myself will help answer the question about the sheriff.

The first thing I can do is actually put myself in circumstances in which people who are different from me exist. I think of a time when I was walking along North Michigan Avenue in Chicago, just north of the Chicago River. That area is commonly known as the Gold Coast of Chicago because of the high-end stores on those six or seven blocks. A homeless person is usually out on each of the blocks, with a foam cup set out for coins and paper money. It occurred to me that I could sit on the sidewalk next to a building and observe the foot and car traffic from the perspective of one of those homeless persons.

I lasted only five minutes. I wanted someone to notice me, catch my eye, say hello. Of the four or five hundred people who walked past me in both directions during those five minutes, none did. I felt neglected, excluded, not worth even so much as a glance. Each minute grew more and more painful until I burst up from the sidewalk and became myself again.

Later, it occurred to me that if I had spent twenty-four hours pretending to be homeless, or even twelve, with only a dollar or two in my pocket, I would have felt firsthand what it feels like not to know when I will be able to eat next or where I will sleep for the night.[38] As it was, those five minutes prodded me to extend my imagination to those twenty-four hours. I was prompted to picture the daily life of a homeless person—the boredom, the uncertainty, the hopelessness at the inability to find a job. And, remarkably, those five minutes opened up my imagination to include numerous other kinds of people who inhabit a world totally different from mine though they live no more than a few miles from me.

I can also read autobiographies and other accounts of people who are different from me. Here I think of the Saturday afternoon forty years ago when my wife randomly bought a book of slave narratives at a garage sale. I was totally unprepared for what I read. I shuddered at the raw beatings. I imagined myself being a slave, unable to extricate myself from slavery yet desperately wanting to. I imagined the dread I would feel at the prospect of having my children sold to a slaveholder in another state, never to see them again. I imagined myself setting out some quiet Saturday night, slogging through backwoods swamps, occasionally catching a glimpse of the North Star as I headed for freedom, intensely fearful of being caught by slave patrols. I also imagined myself being Black now and having in my ancestry, not George Washington and other White heroes of the fledgling United States, but people who had had to endure the horrors of slavery.

Last, I can be proactive in maintaining friendships with people of color I meet. Here the point is not to ask them what it is like to be a person of color in White America, but simply to be friends as equals. Friends listen to each other, and in listening each learns about the other. Each becomes able to picture the experiences the other has, and so the imagination of each is stretched. Here I think of the countless students I have listened to in the dining halls at the colleges at which I have taught and the numerous former students I have listened to at nearby coffee shops. They have included those with a variety of academic abilities, interests, and colors. Listening to their experiences has increased my store of experiences on the basis of which I can imagine other experiences I have not personally had.

Would any of these work with our White sheriff? The best answer, I think, is "It depends." It depends on whether the White sheriff is open to them, or more basically, open to imagining the experiences of other people. This openness, or willingness, is, perhaps, the rock-bottom feature that is needed to have empathy, to apply the Golden Rule, and to be convinced of the need for racial fairness. Without it, these three ways of nurturing moral imagination in oneself will be nonstarters for the White sheriff.

Let us picture the White sheriff being resistant. He stands resolutely with his feet apart. His hands are in front of him, palms facing away from him. The look on his face is one of steely rejection. His whole demeanor says, "Stay away from me." He is not willing to be instructed, does not want to listen to the hurts of others, and especially is not welcoming to having Black people stand before him.

Now let us picture the White sheriff being open. He stands with his hands in front of him, palms up, and elbows at his side. The look on his face is one of welcoming acceptance. He is willing to be instructed. He is ready to listen to those who have been hurt. He is eager to have Black people stand before him and tell him their life stories.

What would it take for the sheriff to give up the stance of resistance and adopt the stance of openness? What would it take for the sheriff to have a change of heart?

Although the three ways of nurturing moral imagination require that one adopt a stance of welcoming acceptance, it might work the other way as well. It might be that the ways of nurturing moral imagination arouse a stance of welcoming acceptance. Let us imagine how this might work with the sheriff.

One day one of his children reports that she has been bullied at school. Our sheriff is incensed. He instantly has angry words with the school principal. He does so on the basis solely of his simple knowledge that his child has been hurt. Later that day, though, the long-forgotten memory of having been bullied as a child pops into his mind. He remembers feeling demeaned because of the derogatory words of the bully. He recalls feeling helpless because the bully was so much bigger than he was. He relives the sense of shame he felt because of the smirks on the faces of the bully's friends. And suddenly he has empathy for his child, not just simple knowledge. He feels his child's helplessness and shame. For the first time in his life, he imagines what it is like for someone else to have painful experiences.

Could the sheriff's empathy for his child awaken an openness in him toward Black people's experiences? Yes, if that empathy prompts him to have empathy for others outside his immediate family, and if it prompts him to recognize that Black people have the same painful feelings that his child has. But, no, if the entrenched Whiteness in him has so much power over him that he is not moved to regard Black people as having painful feelings that result from racial disparities.

In the end, we can only have a hopeful optimism mixed with a residual skepticism. Although some White people may develop their moral imagination in racial ways, some may never do so.

Jonathan
Police Encounters

Jonathan was thirty-six when we talked. He has had numerous racialized experiences, including the police encounters he recounts here. He went to a Christian college in the Midwest and has a master's degree in communication and culture from that college.

MY FIRST RACIAL EXPERIENCE occurred when my family lived in Hawaii for two years. I was in second grade. There was this kid at school who followed me around and called me "Negro." I thought, "What? What does that mean?" I asked my parents, but they didn't explain much. I think they were surprised by how early racialized events had started to occur to me, and they didn't want me to have to deal with that so soon. For the entire time I was at that school, that kid wouldn't call me by my name.

At the time, I didn't know what "Negro" means. But it didn't feel good to be called that, because it isn't my name. I had the sense that it is pejorative, and it definitely made me angry. Later, when I had it explained to me, and after I had read James Baldwin, I learned that being called that is a stand-in so that someone doesn't have to acknowledge Black people as people.

One of the big racialized experiences I have had since then occurred when I was in high school. About seven o'clock one evening, after it had gotten dark, my mom asked me to go get gas in the car so that she wouldn't have to stop on her way to work the next morning. We lived in Zion, Illinois, at the time. While I was inside the gas station paying for the gas, I

Jonathan

noticed police officers in there as well. And as I drove away, one of them followed me. Then I saw three other police cars following the first one. Then four, and ultimately it ended with five.

They stopped me and got into a formation around me. All of their spotlights were on me, so all I saw was the flashing red lights above their cars and the spotlights, like a wall of lights.

One of the police officers got out of his car and came to my window. He wanted to see my license, car registration, and proof of insurance. I gave them to him. He spent some time away, and then all of a sudden several of the other officers came to my car with a drug dog. The dog sniffed for drugs and the other officers checked the spare tire, which was on the back of the Blazer. Then they opened the back doors and checked the back seats, ripping stuff apart. After checking the front seats and the glove compartment, they went back to their cars. When the officer returned with my license and the other two things, he said, "Oh, the reason we stopped you is that you fit the description of someone, and the back light over your license plate was out. So we had to check." I thought, "I had no clue that you required that many people." I wanted to say that, but in situations like that I don't speak other than what I need to say. The back light was working, so that wasn't why I got stopped.

I was enraged. It infuriated me that I could not do anything about the power imbalance.

Another time, when I was a junior in high school, I was talking with a friend of mine on the sidewalk across the street from my house after the school bus had dropped us off there. We were just wrapping up our conversation before going our separate ways when an officer pulled up. We were confused. The officer said, "Hey! I need to see your IDs." "For what?" I asked. "Someone called in that there was a drug deal going on down here," he replied. I said, "I don't know how deductive reasoning works here, but we just got off the school bus and we have backpacks on. So one can infer that we might be students." I was bewildered. How could anyone conclude that a drug deal was going on when you could see that the school bus had just driven away and that we had backpacks on?

The officer would not let us go. He checked our IDs and told us that we could not hang out there. I said, "I live here. There's my house." He said, "You can't be hanging out here."

I was infuriated again. It was one of those scenarios where I have zero clue how someone came to the conclusion that I was a drug dealer unless they were operating from some sense of racial encoding. I should not be judged like a criminal and treated like one simply because I occupy a space with black skin, when I've done nothing wrong, when I'm just existing.

I even asked the officer, "Bro, you know that this is because I'm Black, right? We have done nothing. I'm not allowed to stand on my own street? To have a conversation with another person?" He said, "I have to do this. You guys are loitering." I said, "This is public space!" At that moment I realized that this was not going to go anywhere. His attitude was, "If you talk back to me, you're going to get a ticket." So I let him be.

The most harrowing incident occurred during my freshman year of college. I and three other Black students were at a church rehearsing for a music show we were going to do at the church. One of them was driving the rest of us back to campus. As we were driving, a police car passed us going in the opposite direction. We could see the two officers in the car look at us, their heads following us. We knew. They did a quick U-turn, followed us, and pulled us over on a side street. They went to the driver first. He was a six-foot-five basketball player, so when the officers told him to get out of the car, they reached for their guns, because he was huge. The other one in the front seat was six-two, so that did not make them feel less uncomfortable.

By this time, I had had enough interaction with police to know that I had to be extra cautious. So when one of them said to me, "You need to get out," I said, "My seat belt's buckled." He said, "You need to unbuckle it." I replied, "To do that I have to reach down." He said, "You can reach down to get it." I said, "Here is my hand; you better not shoot me." I raised my left hand up like this [showing me his hand at head level and wiggling the index finger], and I showed him my other hand, like this [showing me his right hand also at head level]. I pushed the seat belt buckle with the index finger of my left hand, then got out. I was a football player, 240 pounds, so the officers were still no less uncomfortable.

After the last of us four got out, they made us take our coats off. This was in January, so we got cold. They searched us, doing a pat-down on our legs first. While they're coming up on our legs, they hit us in the groin. We thought, "Really?! We've given you no friction. We're allowing you to break the law so you can interact with us." It got tense. We were cold, and they were hitting us.

We sat on the curb for fifteen minutes while they searched the car, still without coats on. One of the officers found one of the other students' mom's Bible in the car. He said, "You can't have a Bible." One of us said, "We're allowed to have a Bible." The mood changed quickly. One of the officers said, "You guys can just tell us if you have anything in the car or you can all die drug dealers tonight." One of us said, "There ain't nothing in the car." I said, "Whoa! Whoa! Whoa! You're making the insinuation that you were going to kill us and plant drugs on us. That's what you're telling us." I could tell that the other officer was getting real uncomfortable with what was going on. That one said, "Hey! We need to get out of here."

I had an epiphany when the one officer threatened to kill us and plant drugs on us. It was that narrative matters. At that moment, he was displaying to us that he had a power narrative over us. He could off us right then and, as far as our family and friends and American society would be concerned, we would be a bunch of drug dealers who tried to jump them and then they had to protect themselves. To this day, that has had a profound impact on how I view officer-involved shootings. I cannot unsee, I cannot unexperience, the way that one officer very cavalierly threw out the fact that they could do whatever they wanted to us and everybody would believe them.

5

Black and Wild, Like a Bear
Police Brutality and Moral Perception

IN THE 1991 VIDEO of Rodney King being beaten by four police officers, the Black King is on the ground writhing in pain as he tries to defend himself from the clubs of the White officers. King flails his arms. He groans as another club hits him. The officers could easily secure King with handcuffs, yet they continue to attack King for several agonizing minutes.

Why did they do this?

In his *Look, a Negro!* Robert Gooding-Williams gives an answer to this question when he writes about the trial in which none of the police officers were convicted of using excessive force against King: "The defense attorneys [for Rodney King] elicited testimony from King's assailants that depicted King repeatedly as a bear, and as emitting bear-like groans. In the eyes of the police, and then again in the eyes of the jurors [who acquitted the officers], King's Black body became that of a wild 'Hulk-like' and 'wounded' animal, whose every gesture threatened the existence of civilized society."[39]

The White police officers saw King's Black body as wild and threatening, like a bear that would rise up and swat them with its powerful and perilous paws. They heard King's painful groans as menacing growls. Bears, of course, are scary. Anyone who meets them in the wild, as I have, instinctively tenses up.

Why did the police officers regard King's groans as bear-like growls? Why did they perceive King's prone body as a threatening and dangerous object that needed to be subdued? To answer these questions, we need to look at two features of the officers' perceptions.

(1) The police officers' perceiving was immediate and instinctive. They did not stop to deliberate about how they should think of what they were seeing, but beat King immediately after hearing what sounded to them to be threatening noises. This is how nearly all of us see most everyday objects, such as trees and cars. We nearly always recognize them instantly when we see them. It was the same with the police officers—they instantaneously saw the Black King as dangerous as a wild bear.

(2) The officers' perceiving was also learned. This too is like ordinary perceiving. Children do not automatically know what trees and cars are, but have to learn to see certain shapes as consisting of certain kinds of things. In the same way, the officers went through a process of acquiring what they thought was the knowledge that Black bodies are wild and threatening. This "knowledge" prompted them to see King's twisting, Black body as wild and bear-like. That threatening body had to be subdued before it attacked the officers, indeed, before it attacked the very existence of civilized society.

Although the White officers' perception of the Black King was like ordinary perception in these two ways, it differed in a significant way: it had a moral component. This moral component consisted of an assessment of the worth of what they saw—it was not good like the officers conceived themselves to be; it was not to be trusted; it was able to hurt if not subdued; it was like a threatening bear.

The officers eyes saw only black skin, what everyone else who was there would have seen—one color among others. But their moral assessment of Black people was added to the visual component of the perception. This moral assessment was a lens through which the officers' visual perception was filtered to produce the complex perception of a Black human. It was just as instinctive as their visual perception was, because the moral assessment of being Black had become ingrained in the officers. It had become so much a part of their stance toward Black people that it automatically fused with their visual perception of the color black on a human.

Here are examples of moral perception. You notice that someone at a nearby table in a coffee shop is quietly crying, and you instantly feel empathy for them. Another customer sees the crying but is annoyed at having to be near a person in visible distress. Or you notice an elderly, ill-kempt person stumble and fall on a crowded city street, and you stop to help her up. Others who see what has happened continue on their way, indifferent to the plight of someone who is not generally valued by society.

In each case, you saw what happened differently from the way others saw what happened. You did, of course, visually see the same event that others saw. But your values combined with your visual perception. You have acquired these values over the course of your life, and they shape how you observe people in distress. You perceive people in distress, instantly and without deliberation, in a way that differs from the way in which indifferent others perceive them, also instantly and without deliberation. This is because those others have acquired different values or have been indifferent to certain values.

The police officers who beat Rodney King had acquired values with respect to Black people over the course of their lives. Because they were White, these values undoubtedly included the sense of White normality and superiority that is common among Whites in the United States. This sense affected the way they perceived the Black King as being more like a dangerous animal than a human.

The officers' moral perception of King heightened their sense of being unsafe. Police officers are trained to keep safety as a priority in their encounters with unknown people. But an assessment of safety can be affected by racially biased attitudes. When this is the case, officers are likely to regard themselves as being unsafe more quickly. They are then more likely to use excessive force. Police officers, therefore, cannot absolve themselves simply by saying that they had felt unsafe. This feeling of being unsafe may have been influenced by the prejudicial values they had acquired.

The officers who brutally beat Rodney King would have acquired their values regarding Black people in the numerous subtle and not-so-subtle ways in which nearly everyone in White America acquires them—in their families, schools, neighborhoods, churches, workplaces, and in movies and on television. The officers probably watched the evening news on television, where they could have picked up the belief that Black males are frequently criminal. It has been shown by Jerry Kang that "Blacks are disproportionately portrayed in crime news," which itself disproportionately occupies television news. If the officers had watched movies and shows on television, they would also have picked up the same belief—Martin Gilens has shown that in these too "Blacks are commonly portrayed as criminals."[40]

Christopher Lebron, who cites these facts in his *The Color of Our Shame: Race and Justice in Our Time*, concludes that Black people are viewed by Whites in the United States as having less social value.[41] If this is true, it almost certainly was true of the White police officers who beat Rodney King. It means that they would have instinctively perceived King as threatening and as having less value. They would have literally seen him, without a moment's hesitation, as a wild animal that needed forceful restraint.

This thought is reinforced by one study done by social psychologists, who "have found that the association in ordinary white minds between black Americans and apes remains strong and emotion-laden."[42] This fact means that White police officers are likely to have their moral perceptions of Black Americans formed by this stereotype.

This association between Black people and animals is intensified by the fact that King's skin tone was dark black (really, dark brown), and that those who are dark black are at the far end of the color scale in colorism. Colorism is the belief that people with "white" skin (really, pinkish off white) have more value than those with non-white skin, and further that there are gradations of value among people with non-white skin, those with lighter skin having more value than those with darker skin. Studies have shown that colorism is an international phenomenon.[43] The colorism in American culture, then, would have been picked up by the White police officers and would thus have affected their perception of a writhing, dark-skinned form.

One of the most significant features of moral perception is that the valuational part of it is likely to be unconscious and thus not able to be articulated easily. The valuational part has been ingrained so deeply in people that they are not normally aware of it. It is somewhat like having glasses on—after putting them on, one forgets that they are there. Unlike putting glasses on, though, in moral perception one is not usually aware that certain values are being embedded in oneself. They are simply what one breathes in as one grows up and what one takes in as an adult from the value-laden contexts one inhabits. It is this fact that accounts for the instinctiveness of moral perception—the immediate recognition that someone is in distress or the automatic classifying of someone with black skin as morally inferior.

It is important to say that everyone has moral perceptions, not just White police officers who beat Black Americans. This is because everyone is exposed to the values of the families and cultures of which they are a part. In families in which people who are in distress are cared for, children will grow up being attuned to the signs of distress that people exhibit. In cultures in which women are devalued, men are likely to perceive women as having less value than other men, and some women will as well. Those who inhabit multiracial contexts in which everyone is fully respected and valued are much more likely to have moral perceptions of people who differ from them as fully human and worthy of being respected. Our moral perceptions permeate our daily interactions with others. They have been deeply embedded in us through the common process of absorbing the values that surround us.

This deep embeddedness of values makes it seem as though our moral perceptions are normal and natural. It is this sense of being normal and natural that makes it hard for people to change the way in which they perceive others. Still, moral perceptions are like visual perceptions of physical objects in that perceivers can come to realize that they are mistaken and can unlearn their habit of seeing people in certain ways.

The unlearning of habits, though, can be very difficult, unlike correcting visual perceptions. The latter may simply involve getting closer to what one perceives, whereas the former involves changing attitudes and emotions to which one has become deeply attached and which are not able to be described easily. The difficulty of changing one's emotional attachments is illustrated by the case of children who have been seriously betrayed by an older male and who have come to distrust all older males. That is their instinctive and automatic way of perceiving them. The children's distrust may be able to be dissolved through contacts with older males who prove to be trustworthy, and over a period of years they may be able to change their moral perception of the males they encounter. Despite this change, their initial instinctive distrust may arise from time to time, and they may have to fight it off when in the presence of an older male who has proven to be trustworthy.

The same is true when changing one's racially injurious moral perceptions. Even though one recognizes that they are mistaken, that is not enough to change these automatic and instinctive moral perceptions. To do that, one has to change the deeply embedded attitudes and emotions one has had toward people of different races. This may take years of slow unlearning. Sometimes it may involve battling occasional resurgence of one's former instincts.

The aim of changing one's racially injurious moral perceptions is to perceive people who are different as fully human and deserving of equal respect automatically, instinctively, and immediately whenever one encounters them. The aim is for these moral perceptions to feel natural and normal.

Black and Wild, Like a Bear

The long list of Black people who have been killed by White police officers in the past two decades makes it imperative that police officers' flawed moral perceptions of Black people be corrected. Though it may take time and uncomfortable effort to bring about this change, the process needs to be started, and it needs to be kept up year after year.

The best way to engage in this process is through official programs that all police officers in a particular department participate in. Although individual efforts are good, each police officer needs to know that other officers with whom they work have the same mindset. Otherwise, racially injurious groupthink may take over when two or more White police officers are involved in an encounter with a person of color.

Groupthink occurs when an individual in a group makes a decision based on the urge to conform to the group. Groupthink definitely appears to have been operating in the Rodney King beating. But it could also operate when an individual who is acting alone simply pictures the group of which they are a part being present or simply regards themselves as needing to uphold the modes of conduct of the group. In this way, a police officer who acts alone can still be affected by the urge to conform to the racially injurious modes of conduct of fellow police officers.

So those racially injurious modes of conduct need to be changed among whole police departments, not just by individual police officers, by themselves, one by one. And because racially injurious modes of conduct are brought about by racially injurious moral perceptions, those perceptions need to be changed as well.

With unbiased moral perceptions of race, White police officers would not be so quick to kill Black Americans, and White juries would be more impartial in their deliberations about cases involving Black victims.

Lest it be thought that the only approach to changing police brutality is first to change the moral perceptions of police officers, it needs to be said that things can work in the reverse order as well. In fact, the best approach may sometimes be to work on conduct first, as the Center for Policing Equity does.[44] Their aim is to help city police departments reduce the disproportionate use of force against Black Americans and other people of color by helping those departments set standards of conduct. It is a known fact that a change of conduct can change attitudes. The authors of *Principles of Social Psychology* state, "It turns out that if we engage in a behavior, and particularly one that we had not expected that we would have, our thoughts and feelings toward that behavior are likely to change."[45] So when police officers change their conduct against people of color through enforced departmental policy, that is likely to change their attitudes toward them along with their moral perceptions of them. And this, in turn, will help cement the conduct.

6

Black Power, White Power

Two Events

IN JUNE OF 1966, a large group of marchers made their way from Memphis, Tennessee, to Jackson, Mississippi, on a "March of Fear." The point of the march was to advocate for Black people's ability to walk unscathed through the state of Mississippi. About halfway to Jackson, in Greenwood, Mississippi, the marchers—1,500 of them—paused for a rally, where the fiery Stokely Carmichael declared to them, "We been saying freedom for six years and we ain't got nothin'. What we got to start saying now is Black power! We want Black power."[46] When Carmichael yelled, "What do you want?" the crowd responded with "Black power!" It soon became a chant: "We want Black power! We want Black power!"[47]

Carmichael's speech that night was a historic moment in the Civil Rights Movement. Until then, the slogan had been "Freedom now," which had been used by Martin Luther King Jr. and his associates. Afterwards, "Black power" became the slogan of those who, like Carmichael, had become impatient with the slowness of progress toward racial equity.

On a warm summer afternoon in the mid-1990s, I drove to Rockford, in northern Illinois, where a local chapter of the Ku Klux Klan was to hold a rally at the Rockford courthouse. I planned to be part of the protest.

I arrived in Rockford in time to join a group of demonstrators marching around the streets of Rockford. Just before the Klan was to speak, I passed through the metal detectors that police had set up at the entrance to the area in which anti-Klan demonstrators were allowed. This area was about two hundred feet from the steps of the county courthouse and was solidly barricaded with A-frame wood barricades. A line of forty or fifty police officers, fully equipped with helmets and anti-riot gear, stood stiffly in front of the barricade.

The anti-Klan area soon became filled with a hundred or so protesters plus roving police with thick wood sticks and large plastic pepper sprayers. Though the Klan had not arrived, the protesters were shouting and swaying. When the Klan members arrived, the crowd's shouting increased dramatically. I moved away so I could hear what the Klan speakers were saying. They spoke from the middle of the courthouse stairs, in front of a row of eight to ten fellow Klan members. None of the Klan people wore their customary White hoods, and they included both women and men.

At the end of one of the speeches, the speaker raised his right arm, clenched his fist, and yelled into the microphone, "White power! White power! White power!"[48]

The question these two incidents raise is whether Carmichael and the Klan speaker had the same concept of power in mind when they uttered their slogans. Did the White supremacists and Black civil rights protesters agree on the idea, albeit with a different stance toward it? Or did they have different concepts of power? Let us look at Carmichael's "Black power" first. (He later changed his name to Kwame Ture, but I shall refer to him as Carmichael, as that was his name during the 1960s.)

Two Senses of Power

Carmichael's new slogan was commonly interpreted as a call for violence. This interpretation was not without a basis in what Carmichael stated in his June 16 Greenwood speech: "We have begged the president. We've begged the federal government—that's all we've been doing, begging and begging. It's time we stand up and take over. Every courthouse in Mississippi ought to be burned down tomorrow to get rid of the dirt and the mess."[49]

Carmichael, however, did not mention violent resistance a year later in his and Charles V. Hamilton's book, *Black Power: The Politics of Liberation*. There he and Hamilton specifically define Black power as self-determination: "Black people must come together and do things for themselves. They must achieve self-identity and self-determination."[50] This self-determination, they say, "means proper representation and sharing of control." It means "an effective share in the total power of the society."[51] In different words, Carmichael and Hamilton think of Black power as having what is rightly due anyone, namely, control over their own lives.

This control is linked to equality of opportunity. You cannot have control over your life if you do not have opportunities to vote or live where you wish or have a good education or participate in political processes. So Carmichael and Hamilton's call for Black power includes a call for equal opportunities.

Some people, however, have interpreted their call for Black power as a demand for Black supremacy: "Some observers have labeled those who advocate Black Power as racists; they have said that the call for self-identification and self-determination is 'racism in reverse' or 'black supremacy.'"[52] Carmichael and Hamilton explicitly reject the sense of power as having domination over others. The control they want is over their own lives, not that of others: "The ultimate values and goals are not domination or exploitation of other groups. . . . The goal of black self-determination and black self-identity—Black Power—is full participation in the decision-making processes affecting the lives of black people."[53] They deny that they are racists, because "racism is not merely exclusion on the basis of race but exclusion for the purpose of subjugating or maintaining subjugation."[54] They are not advocating that Black people subjugate White people. They do not want to restrict the right of White people to vote or the right to live where they wish. They are not calling for Black Americans to have superior schools or total control of local, state, or federal political power. None of their calls for Black power are meant for Black folks to have more power than White folks have.

The two senses of power involved in Carmichael and Hamilton's statements are self-determination and domination. The first is having control of one's own life. The second is having control over other people's lives. Carmichael and Hamilton adopt the first and reject the second. It is self-determination they want, not domination. They do not want to take away the self-determination of White Americans, just their domination.

The Klan people in the Rockford rally did not specify which sense of power they were adopting. But, given the history of the KKK, it is pretty evident that they were concerned with domination. They wanted to maintain their domination over people of color, specifically over Black Americans. They wanted what White supremacists and White nationalists have always wanted: to maintain a hierarchy of power with White people at the top of the hierarchy.

Things are not so simple, however, as merely pointing out that there are two senses of power, for there are connections between the two senses, and there are truths about power that need unpacking.

A Connection

Perhaps the most obvious truth about the two senses of power in the racial context we are looking at is that White people will have to give up their domination of people of color if people of color are to be able to exercise self-determination. In different words, if White people retain their power of domination, then Black people will not have the ability to live their own lives. They will be unduly restricted.

Carmichael and Hamilton no doubt realized this. They realized that as long as White Americans hold on to their dominant control over jobs, housing, education, and political positions, Black Americans cannot exercise their right to self-determination and cannot have equal opportunities. They cannot have control over their own lives in these domains, for White folks will be limiting the opportunities Black folks have in them. If White people want the ability to live in neighborhoods that are all White, that is, to dominate who lives in those neighborhoods, then Black people cannot exercise their right of self-determination to live in them. If Whites want to be dominant in every political position, national, state, and local, then Blacks cannot exercise their right to a fair share of political power.

The Klan people probably also realized this connection between the two senses of power. Their domination would have to be given up if Black people were to exercise their right to self-determination.

Klan people, however, desperately do not want to give up that power, which is why they were so passionate in their declarations of "White power!" The truth is that the desire to maintain the power to dominate can be intense.

The Desire for Power

This truth can be stated more strongly: having the power to dominate is extremely alluring. It lures from childhood to old age. It seduces one into exercising power over others in little ways and big ways, in everyday, personal interactions and larger social ways. It does so partly because having this kind of power beguiles one into thinking that one is somebody, that one is better than others. And everyone wants to think of themselves as better than someone else. This desire often lurks below the level of full awareness. It can motivate people even though it is not fully conscious.

In a racial context, the desire for domination lures White people into exercising control over people of color, especially Black people, because it entices them into thinking that they are superior to Black people, that is, that Black people are inferior to them. Sometimes it lures White people into regarding Black people as less than human, especially during the era of slavery and lynching, as David Livingstone Smith describes at length in his *Less than Human: Why We Demean, Enslave, and Exterminate Others*: "The dehumanization of African Americans did not end with the creation of a new nation in 1776, or with the abolition of slavery in 1865. Books and pamphlets published during the latter part of the nineteenth and early twentieth centuries continued to assert that they were beasts."[55] It is not hard to imagine Klan people adopting the same sentiment.

It would not be fair to declare that White people are the only ones who are lured by the power to dominate. Everyone is, including people of color. If a current minority group were in the majority, some might well be so attracted to the power to dominate as to be like Klan people. It is certainly possible, though, for anyone, Black, White, or Brown, to feel the lure of domination and yet to resist it. There are, in fact, numerous Black, White, and Brown people who do so. Carmichael and Hamilton themselves explicitly disavowed that the power they wanted was to dominate Whites.

Given the ubiquity of the desire for domination, it would be the honest thing for all humans to say that though they have felt the lure of domination, they reject it and want never to act in accordance with it. It certainly is the honest thing for Klan members to say. They should repent—confess that they have acted out of the wrongful desire to dominate and change their behavior so that they no longer advocate for domination or act in dominant ways. It is the honest thing for other White people to say, myself included—all of us who have been recipients of undue privilege because we are White, a privilege that amounts to economic, political, educational, and social dominance.

It is also true that everyone desires self-determination. Everyone wants to be able to live their own lives. This desire too starts at a young age and remains until death. Young children want to tie their own shoelaces.

Teens want to be more independent. Adults do not want to be unduly restricted in what they do, either by governments, by domineering employers, or by uncooperative neighbors. The desire is strong, sometimes fierce. People have left their homelands to seek self-determination. Wars have been fought to acquire it. The Civil Rights Era was motivated by it. The desire is, of course, good.

The desire for self-determination is good because self-determination is a basic right of all humans. It is a *basic* right because other rights cannot be enjoyed without having self-determination. Having it, in different words, is necessary for having a good and satisfying life.

Sometimes people whose right to self-determination has been restricted need to be encouraged to desire the right more strongly. With a strong desire for self-determination, people will be more likely to demand that it be respected by those who have curtailed it. With his calls for Black power, Stokely Carmichael was encouraging people to demand the right to self-determination.

In contrast to the desire for self-determination, the desire to dominate is illegitimate. This is so because having control over another person conflicts with their right of self-determination. There are exceptions to this, of course, such as for parents of small children. But when the desire to dominate is not grounded in a legitimate reason, it should be resisted. This includes the desire to feel superior to others as humans. It is a character flaw to nurture this desire, because it is a sign of excessive self-centeredness. In racial contexts, it is a sign of excessive racial self-centeredness, which is what the desire for White superiority consists of: "We are better humans because we have white skin."

Conception of Oneself

This last sentiment is often tied to self-identity, that is, to the conception one has of oneself. This is especially true of the power to dominate. Those with this power regard it as central to their identity.

It is helpful to look at James Baldwin's comments about identity again. Writing about White Americans, he observes that "they have had to believe for many years, and for innumerable reasons, that black men are inferior to white men."[56] Given that this is so, he continues, there would be a grave danger if Black Americans were ever to become equal to White Americans: "The danger, in the minds of most White Americans, is the loss of their identity."[57]

This loss, Baldwin declares, would be catastrophic to White folks: "The black man has functioned in the white man's world as a fixed star, as an immovable pillar: and as he moves out of his place, heaven and earth are shaken to their foundations."[58] It would be catastrophic because White Americans have been so heavily invested in their identity as being superior to Black Americans that to undermine that superiority with equality would be tantamount to undermining their very existence.

It may have been that Carmichael and Hamilton also noticed this connection between White power and self-conception. If they did, in demanding self-determination for Black people they were demanding not only that White people give up their power to dominate but also that White people make a radical change in their self-conception. And if the Klan members were aware of the connection, they would have felt that their very existence was being threatened by Black demands for self-determination. They would have felt this because a central part of their being who they were—White Americans—included having dominance over Black Americans.

Having the power of self-determination can also be central to the conception of oneself. Carmichael and Hamilton may have been acknowledging this when, in the above quote, they refer both to "self-identity and self-determination": "Black people must come together and do things for themselves. They must achieve self-identity and self-determination."[59] Carmichael and Hamilton do not make it clear whether they think there is a connection between self-identity and self-determination. There clearly is, though. Enjoying the right to self-determination enhances one's self-conception. And when someone's right of self-determination is severely restricted, their conception of themselves can be severely harmed.

Think of someone who is repeatedly not allowed to make her own decisions in a context in which it would be normal for her to do so. The message she would pick up is that she cannot be trusted. And this would make her feel less worthy, less valuable as a person. The same is true in racial contexts. The message people of color can pick up when constantly having their right to self-determination restricted is that they have less value than White people. This harm to their self-conception could bring depression and a sense of giving up—"Why should I try if I know that the forces against me are too strong?" "Is it worth the energy to push against the powers that be, knowing that I probably will fail?"

No doubt some people of color would resist the message of inferiority and conceive of themselves as having worth despite the constant messages to the contrary. They would battle those messages. They would defy the damaging judgment that White domination conveys to them. They would believe in themselves. But now we can ask, could anyone engage in such an internal battle without feeling exhaustion from time to time? Almost certainly not. This too is a harm, a harm that could negatively affect one's self-conception.

One last thought on self-identity: the intense desire for domination, along with the effect of White domination on White self-conception, explains, though does not excuse, why White people are sometimes so adamant and forceful about retaining their privileged position in US culture. If that position were destroyed, it would destroy their racially superior conception of themselves, which would, in essence, destroy their sense of self.

Replacement

I said earlier that Stokely Carmichael and Charles Hamilton declared that they did not want to curtail the self-determination of White folks. Their aim was only to defeat White domination. However, there is a question of whether the self-determination of White people would *in fact* be curtailed if Black people were to be granted more of their right to self-determination. It is certain that White *domination* would have to be curtailed, as I mentioned above, but would White *self-determination* also have to be curtailed? In different words, would White Americans have fewer opportunities to do things if Black Americans had the ability to do more things? Would Blacks replace Whites?

It seems fairly certain that most White people who have an explicit sense of dominance over Black people *believe* not only that their dominance would be undone but also that their right to self-determination would be restricted if Black people were allowed to exercise more self-determination. Some jobs would be acquired by Blacks that Whites could have. Some scholarships to colleges, medical schools, and law schools would be granted to Blacks instead of to Whites.

It also seems fairly certain that most White people who have a sense of their dominance over Black people believe that Black *domination* would replace their own domination so that they would become subservient. In 1880s Georgia, Donald Mathews writes, fear of "Negro Domination" led to the defeat of an interracial coalition for racial reform. And in 1890s

Georgia, Mathews continues, the fear of "Negro supremacy" again defeated attempts at racial reform.[60]

One of the starkest instances of this replacement fear occurred during the disturbance on August 11–12, 2017, in Charleston, Virginia. White nationalists rallied to protest the removal of the statue of Confederate General Robert E. Lee. As they marched through the streets of Charleston, they chanted, "You will not replace us! Jews will not replace us!" Counterprotesters showed up and chanted, "No KKK!" In the melee that ensued, one person was killed. After the disturbance was quelled, a reporter was able to interview half a dozen White nationalists, who explained why they were rallying. In one video clip, a young White mother, who was holding her two young children while sitting on a well-tended lawn, declared that she would not be averse to seeing Jews shot. "I do not want them to replace my children," she declared.

These beliefs do not settle the question of whether the exercise of Black or Jewish or any other non-White self-determination would *in fact* curtail White self-determination. Those who believe it would are assuming that the domains in which Black Americans would exercise their self-determination are zero-sum, that is, ones in which what is gained by one person will be lost by another. The truth, however, is that it is not easy to determine whether any of the common domains—educational, political, employment, housing—are zero-sum. Some might be, but many almost certainly are not. And it is also true that replacement is rarely all or nothing. It comes in degrees.

Consider scholarships. If a college, law school, or medical school has a set number of scholarships to give, then giving scholarships to Black applicants would reduce the number of scholarships given to White applicants. This looks as though it is a straightforward replacement. But two considerations undermine this assessment. The first is that if all the scholarships had previously gone to White applicants, the replacement would involve undoing White *domination,* not White self-determination. The second is that there are more colleges, law schools, and medical schools to which White people can apply. The replacement assessment for just one of these institutions loses its force when a wider array of institutions is involved.

But now consider this wider array. Suppose all of them, in the aggregate, have a set number of scholarships. Is this not a zero-sum situation? It certainly looks as though it is. But here, again, there are two responses. The first is that it is, indeed, somewhat closer to a zero-sum situation. But hardly anything is ever completely zero-sum. In the case of a denied scholarship, White applicants still have options: apply again the following year, work while going to college, obtain a loan. These are options that other scholarship-rejected applicants, including Black and Brown applicants, can pursue, and indeed have pursued. Moreover, in the US's White-dominated culture, what White students regard as entitlement to self-determination has been almost entirely acquired unjustly. This is so because White people have almost always had a disproportionate amount of educational opportunities because of their social and political domination. So the situation is not that of Black self-determination replacing true White self-determination, but of Black self-determination replacing *unjustly gained* White self-determination. Unjustly gained White self-determination, however, is really White domination. This means that it is not a situation in which both Black people and White people are exercising true self-determination.

If there were such a situation, with truly equal opportunities, would the exercise of non-White self-determination restrict the exercise of White self-determination? The answer is impossible to give, because the degree of replacement is almost always impossible to estimate. If a non-White person were to park in the last parking spot in a parking lot, yes, that would exclude White people from parking *in that lot*. But there are usually other parking spots elsewhere. If a non-White person started a new business, or if a great deal of non-White people started new businesses, then, yes, it may be that some people, White and non-White, would make their purchases at those businesses, thus causing White businesses to acquire less wealth than they formerly did. Here the replacement level is a good deal lower than in the parking lot case, for there are numerous economic variables at play. The same is true of acquiring jobs. It may be that a non-White person's acquiring a certain job means that a White person will not have that particular job. But, because the economic variables are so numerous, it may be that the effect of the non-White person's having that particular job will actually increase opportunities for self-determination for both non-White people and White people, instead of decreasing them.

From these considerations, we can conclude that the replacement worry of White folks need not be high. But another consideration shows that it is, in fact, entirely misplaced.

Misplaced

If it were true that non-White self-determination curtails White self-determination, then it would also be true that White self-determination curtails non-White self-determination. It goes both ways. So it is as legitimate for non-White people to worry about being replaced as it is for White people to worry about it, given that non-White people and White people should have equal opportunity to exercise self-determination. There should be parity of concern, which is to say that there should be equal concern for non-White and White self-determination. It is illegitimate for White Americans to be concerned only about their own self-determination power. That is indicative of self-centeredness. Their concern for self-determination should be accompanied by concern for non-White self-determination. It is not self-centeredness, though, for non-White Americans to issue calls for non-White self-determination power, because that power has been curtailed to varying degrees in different domains by White dominance.

It is sometimes pointed out that calls by non-White Americans for equal *self-determination* power in economic, social, and political contexts are likely to be seen by White Americans who have dominance power as calls for non-White *domination* power. This failure to see the difference between self-determination and dominance may be what motivated negative White reaction to Stokely Carmichael's call for Black power. White people who reacted negatively to this call did not see that they were blinded by their own sense of dominance. Equal right to self-determination was not part of their moral outlook. Their own sense of dominance was so ingrained in their conception of themselves that they regarded the call for Black self-determination as striking at the core of who they were.

One might wonder here whether there ever was a system in which self-determination power was equally distributed. The lure of domination power through wealth, political power, and racial superiority is so strong that a system of truly equal opportunities for all seems unlikely. This pessimistic fact, however, need not undermine striving for more equality. Perfect equality may be impossible, but greater equality is not.

Black Power Matters

Black self-determination power matters because without it there will be no racial equity. It also matters because it is needed for a good and true

The Uneasy Conscience of a White Christian

self-conception for both Black people and White people. Although White dominance in the United States has diminished some since Carmichael and Hamilton's book was published in 1967, it still exists. So calls for Black self-determination power are still needed. As long as any degree of White dominance persists, Black self-determination will not be equal to that of White people. And without equal levels of self-determination, or at least mostly equal levels, the United States will remain highly racialized. Racial tensions will remain.

Devlin

Systems

Devlin was thirty-six when I talked with him. He is pastor of a church in Massachusetts.

When I was five years old, there was a knock on the front door of our house one day, and my sister opened the door without asking who was there. It was a group of armed Black men. They charged in, used extension cords to tie us up, and burglarized our house.

I wasn't tied up because I was so young. But they beat my adult cousin, who was visiting us, and they tried to get my mother to lie down on her stomach, but they couldn't because she was pregnant with my brother.

It was very traumatizing. The most traumatizing thing for me was that they drank my juice from the refrigerator. I thought, "Give me my juice back!" That was all the sense I could make of the horrible thing that was happening.

That night, two police officers, one Black and one White, came to our house to take a statement. After my mom described to them what happened, the Black police officer said, "Why would they want to rob you? You must have been doing something wrong. There must be something happening in your house that prompted them to come to your house. So what are you doing?"

They blamed it on us that we were burglarized. I thought, "Wait! That feels wrong. We're supposed to be protected, not blamed." It felt extremely

The Uneasy Conscience of a White Christian

unjust and kind of abusive. We were the victims—why would you kick people who were down? Why would you blame the victims for what happened to them?

I also felt that what the police officer said had more to do with the fact that we were Black and that we lived in a Black neighborhood than anything else.

Since that day, I have never been comfortable with police officers protecting me and my family. They were an authority structure that was not for us, adversaries I could not trust. Whenever I have seen authority after that day, I have sensed that it is carrying out the orders of White people. In that incident at age five, I was awakened to systems of injustice and unfairness and inequality.

Later, I came to realize that the educational disparity between the high school I went to and other high schools had a racial dimension. Of the 3,000 or so in my high school, I could count the number of Whites on one hand.

There were 1,200 students classified as seniors in my graduating class, but only 301 graduated, and by graduation day only 40 had been accepted into college. The acceptance letters of those 40 were posted on the wall at the school, including mine. At the time, I thought, "Oh, great!" But when I got to college and met my future wife, I realized just how bad these numbers were. At the predominantly White high school she went to, in a northern suburb of Chicago, all but one graduating senior went to college.

This was when I recognized that the educational system I had been part of had failed me and left me at a disadvantage. I was in the top 10 in my high school class with a 3.9 grade point average. I had taken Advanced Placement classes in mathematics, English, and science. Yet after three attempts. I could not score well on the National College Entrance Exam. I did not learn how to diagram a sentence until I took Greek in college, something I should have learned in grade school. There was a wide disparity between my ability to succeed and my preparation to succeed. Another system had let me down.

My lack of preparation wounded my pride some, because I had thought I was ready for college. But I had to struggle when I got to college. That was embarrassing and humbling. I stopped speaking in classes because I didn't trust that I was smart enough. That was even more clear when I got to seminary. I didn't know whether what I had to say in class would be good enough.

I still struggle with not feeling good enough. I still feel that I have to try to prove that I am worthy. I mastered what was put in front of me, but what if what was put in front of me wasn't what I needed? I can't trust that I was prepared for the White places I was later put into. The reality of the educational system in the United States is that White students have advantages that Black students do not have. No matter how hard I had worked, students who went to White high schools would be seen as having more potential than me.

After I got a Master of Divinity degree and a master's degree in bioethics, I served on the pastoral staff of a church that prided itself as being multicultural. It had a lot of diversity in it, though I was the only person of color on the pastoral staff. The people in the church made my wife and me feel that we were beloved and accepted. Our music approach, our style, our preaching style, and our leadership style all made people of color feel comfortable going to the church. It was part of a denomination that was predominantly White, and it had a sister denomination that was predominately Black.

Shortly after the Black Lives Matter movement started in 2013, the churches in the sister denomination were going to have a Black Lives Matter Sunday, and our denomination was asked to stand in solidarity by observing it too. I called the senior pastor of my church and asked, "Are we going to do this? Can we do something?" He said that our church would not be doing anything. I asked him why. He said, "Because we have several police officers who attend our church." I replied, "You also have African Americans in the church, and you have one on staff." He responded, "Yes, but I don't want to offend the police officers."

His response stung. It told me where the values of the senior pastor sat. He did not want to affirm the feelings of the African Americans in the church or the person of color on the pastoral staff. The commitment I had given the church over a number of years did not matter enough.

This hurt me much more than overtly racist events. People often make the assumption that what hurts Black people most and what is the most scary and hardest to deal with is the White supremacists, the white-hooded individuals who utter hateful words. But Black folks know what to do with those people. We know where to place them. We know how to avoid them. We know how to be safe emotionally regarding them. However, when someone close to you, whom you trust, and who says they care for you, shows ignorance and bias and has no openness to learn from the people of color who are standing right by them, that hurts much more.

For my wife and me, this painful moment made us feel that we were on our way out of that church. Even though my wife had grown up in it, and even though I had served it for five or six years, there was a level of unsafety, a level of betrayal, in that one moment. It was too much to overcome. We stayed for two more years, doing as much as we could to bring about change and deepening our involvement in ministry and service, until we felt called to move to Massachusetts to plant a church there.

What we felt at that moment was only exacerbated by subsequent events. A Black man—George Floyd—is murdered on national television and you still don't see me? Kids are locked in cages and you still don't understand?

Sometimes my White friends told me, a Black man, what it means to be Black in the United States. To me, this represents a White privilege that is appalling. I don't understand how people who have never walked in the shoes of someone of color can have the audacity to speak as though they are experts on what African Americans have suffered. They need to stop talking and start listening, as Proverbs says: "Be slow to speak. Be quick to listen." It couldn't be simpler than that. To do the opposite is downright arrogant and drenched in privilege.

Sometimes friends from the Christian college I went to have done the same thing. I thought I had a community, a family, at the college, which had been a fellowship of believers. I had worshipped with them, prayed with them, lived with them. But now it feels as though they were wolves in sheep's clothing. I no longer feel safe in the place I invested so much of my energy, heart, and faith. I struggle to think that the church body is safe. Black folks will have safety only when it is proven.

7

Inhabiting Every Nook and Cranny of American Life

THE CAB DRIVER WAS talkative. In a monologue about presidential politics, he declared, "Civil rights is in the past. We need to let that go and talk about the business of living now."

I wanted to give him some facts that show that the civil rights of Black and Brown Americans are still not fully respected, but I couldn't call to mind anything specific. In fact, I later thought, all I had was the generalized belief that though some progress had been made since the Civil Rights Era, there is still long way to go, plus knowledge of a few recent, highly publicized racially injurious incidents.

So when I got home, I found a number of reputable studies on the Internet that document current racial disparities in the United States, plus articles with descriptions of racially injurious behavior involving individuals. The studies and descriptions include a variety of domains not typically represented in well-known news stories. They show that racially injurious behavior in the United States is not limited to a small number of mean-spirited individuals but reaches into nearly every aspect of everyday living. In the words of George Yancy, it "inhabits every nook and cranny of American life."[61] Racially injurious behavior is not just a police brutality issue or a segregation affair.

Along with the racial microaggressions documented in chapter 9, the statistics and stories in this chapter show that the issues discussed in this book are important. Without knowing at least a little of the "current racial landscape,"[62] one is not likely to be convinced that it is necessary to talk about the effect of racial socialization or the harm of Whiteness to oneself. The same is true of Black and White power and the possibility of church integration. These have a high priority just because of widespread racially injurious behavior.

This chapter and chapter 9 also show that White self-reflection is not the only way to learn about race. Listening to the experiences of people of color is needed just as much, if not more so.

Statistics can seem dry and abstract. But behind each of the following statistics are individuals whose lives are affected. For several of the statistics, I supply an account of how an individual Black or Brown person has been hurt. It is easy to imagine that this is so for each of the other statistics.

Statistics

Acquiring jobs: "A new study released by Georgetown University in part refutes the notion that African Americans and Latinxs can improve their socioeconomic standing just by going to college. According to the study, between 1991 and 2016, Black and Latino Americans increased their likelihood of obtaining and maintaining a good job, but their white peers still disproportionately hold better jobs compared to their overall employment."[63]

Childhood of Black girls: "It's long been suspected that black girls are perceived as more adult-like and less innocent than white girls in school and other environments, and a new report offers further confirmation that this is the case. According to participants in the Georgetown study . . . , 'when Black girls express strong or contrary views, adults view them as challenging authority or, more fundamentally, simply assume a girl's character is just plain "bad."' . . . This bias also likely plays a role in the increasing use of discipline against black girls in the classroom, by law enforcement, and in interactions with authority figures, even though they are no more likely to misbehave than white girls."[64]

- Samaya, a Black girl, age twelve, reports that once her teacher got "super duper mad and dragged me by the chair, yelled at the other kids to move as she was dragging me, and dragged me all the way outside." When she was in second grade, she says, "everything I did, the slightest bit of doing something wrong, like a normal seven-year-old would do, like getting up or speaking without getting called on, would result in getting into big trouble."[65]

Daily discrimination targeting Black adolescents: "Persistent racial discrimination targeting Black adolescents contributes to increased psychological symptoms, increased substance use, decreased academic achievement, and increased physiological problems among these youth (e.g., inflammation, high blood pressure)."[66]

The death penalty: Between January 17, 1977, and June 5, 2021, "more than 75 percent of death row defendants who have been executed were sentenced to death for killing white victims, even though in society as a whole about half of all homicide victims are African American." As of October 1, 2020, 41.60 percent of the death row population was Black even though Blacks are about 13 percent of the US population. Between 1976 and September 24, 2020, there were 21 executions for murder when there was a White defendant and a Black victim, but 296 executions for murder when there was a Black defendant and a White victim.[67]

Drug arrests and incarceration: "Black people comprise 13 percent of the U.S. population, and are consistently documented by the U.S. government to use drugs at similar rates to people of other races. But [in 2015] Black people comprise 29 percent of those arrested for drug law violations, and nearly 40 percent of those incarcerated in state or federal prison for drug law violations. Similarly, Latinos make up 18 percent of the U.S. population, but comprise 38 percent of people incarcerated in federal prisons for drug offenses."[68]

Educational achievement: "Many factors contribute to the achievement gap [between Black students and White students], including home and neighborhood environments and school factors unrelated to teachers' performance. But one dynamic is becoming impossible to ignore: Notable differences in the way black students are treated by teachers and school administrators. Research shows that compared with white students, black students are more likely to be suspended or expelled, less likely to be placed in gifted programs and subject to lower expectations from their teachers. . . . In many cases, such differences in treatment aren't malicious or intentional. Some disparities arise from cultural misunderstandings or unintentional 'implicit biases' that unknowingly affect our thoughts and behaviors."[69]

Home ownership: The percentage of households in the United States who owned homes was 63.9 percent for the third quarter of 2017, and among people of color it was 46.6 percent. The percentages were 72.5 for Whites, 42.7 for Blacks, and 46.0 for Hispanics.[70]

Housing advertising on Facebook: "Facebook unlawfully discriminates based on race, color, national origin, religion, familial status, sex, and disability by restricting who can view housing-related ads on Facebook's platforms and across the internet.... 'Facebook is discriminating against people based upon who they are and where they live,' said HUD [Housing and Urban Development] Secretary Ben Carson. 'Using a computer to limit a person's housing choices can be just as discriminatory as slamming a door in someone's face.'"[71]

Incarceration: "Blacks have long outnumbered Whites in U.S. prisons. But a significant decline in the number of black prisoners has steadily narrowed the gap over the past decade, according to new data from the Bureau of Justice Statistics." Still, "the racial and ethnic makeup of U.S. prisons continues to look substantially different from the demographics of the country as a whole. In 2017, blacks represented 12 percent of the U.S. adult population but 33 percent of the sentenced prison population. Whites accounted for 64 percent of adults but 30 percent of prisoners. And while Hispanics represented 16 percent of the adult population, they accounted for 23 percent of inmates.... In 2017, there were 1,549 black prisoners for every 100,000 black adults—nearly six times the imprisonment rate for whites (272 per 100,000) and nearly double the rate for Hispanics (823 per 100,000)."[72]

Juries: "Today in America, there is perhaps no arena of public life or governmental administration where racial discrimination is more widespread, apparent, and seemingly tolerated than in the selection of juries. Nearly 135 years after Congress enacted the 1875 Civil Rights Act to eliminate racially discriminatory jury selection, the practice continues, especially in serious criminal and capital cases."[73]

"The state of implicit bias research today indicates that jury verdicts regarding Black parties are inherently unfair.... Implicit bias impacts how individuals perceive and react to the world in all areas, including the courtroom. Research indicates that implicit bias makes its way into jury deliberations and accurately predicts the associations jurors make between a defendant's guilt and her race. Specifically, jurors are more likely to associate guilt with a Black defendant than a White defendant."[74]

Killed by police: "African American men and women, American Indian/Alaska Native men and women, and Latino men face higher lifetime risk of being killed by police than do their white peers. . . . Latina women and Asian/Pacific Islander men and women face lower risk of being killed by police than do their white peers. Risk is highest for black men. . . . For young men of color, police use of force is among the leading causes of death."[75]

Life expectancy in the United States: In 2017, the life expectancy in the United States was lowest for Black males and highest for Hispanic females. The average life expectancy was 78.6 years for all races, 78.8 years for Whites, 75.3 years for Blacks, and 81.8 years for Hispanics. It was 81.1 years for all females, 81.2 years for White females, 78.5 years for Black females, and 84.3 for Hispanic females. It was 76.1 years for all males, 76.4 years for White males, 71.9 years for Black males, and 79.1 years for Hispanic males.[76]

Maternal mortality: "For 2011–2015, the national PRMR [pregnancy-related mortality ratio] was 17.2 per 100,000 live births. Non-Hispanic black (black) women and American Indian/Alaska Native women had the highest PRMRs (42.8 and 32.5, respectively), 3.3 and 2.5 times as high, respectively, as the PRMR for non-Hispanic white (white) women (13.0)."[77]

"Unconscious bias can affect quality of care, according to NPR's 2017 investigative report. NPR [National Public Radio] and ProPublica collected 200 stories from African American mothers and found that unconscious bias in health care was a 'constant theme.'"[78]

- Shalon, a black women living in Atlanta, collapsed and died from complications of high blood pressure three weeks after giving birth to her first child. She was thirty-six. She had earned two master's degrees and a PhD and had been a researcher at the Centers for Disease Control and Prevention. At the Center, she had been studying "how people's limited health options were leading to poor health outcomes." With her death, her parents lost the last of their three children.[79]

Media crime coverage: "Many media outlets reinforce the public's racial misconceptions about crime by presenting African Americans and Latinos differently than whites—both quantitatively and qualitatively. Television news programs and newspapers over-represent racial minorities as crime suspects and whites as crime victims."[80]

Median household income: The median household income in the United States for 2016 was $80,001 for White people, $49,000 for Black people, $50,000 for American Indians and Alaska Natives, $96,000 for Asian Americans, $67,950 for Native Hawaiians and other Pacific Islanders, and $56,000 for Hispanic Americans.[81]

Medical intervention: "In 2005, the Institute of Medicine—a not-for-profit, non-governmental organization that now calls itself the National Academy of Medicine (NAM)—released a report documenting that the poverty in which black people disproportionately live cannot account for the fact that black people are sicker and have shorter life spans than their white complements. . . . Scores of studies buttress NAM's findings by documenting that providers are less likely to deliver effective treatments to people of color when compared to their white counterparts—even after controlling for characteristics like class, health behaviors, comorbidities, and access to health insurance and health care services."[82]

"An algorithm widely used in US hospitals to allocate health care to patients has been systematically discriminating against black people, a sweeping analysis has found. The study, published in *Science* on October 24, [2019], concluded that the algorithm was less likely to refer black people than white people who were equally sick to programs that aim to improve care for patients with complex medical needs. Hospitals and insurers use the algorithm and others like it to help manage care for about 200 million people in the United States each year."[83]

Names: "We perform a field experiment to measure racial discrimination in the labor market. We respond with fictitious resumes to help-wanted ads in Boston and Chicago newspapers. To manipulate perception of race, each resume is assigned either a very African American sounding name or a very White sounding name. The results show significant discrimination against African American names: White names receive 50 percent more callbacks for interviews. We also find that race affects the benefits of a better resume. For White names, a higher quality resume elicits 30 percent more callbacks whereas for African Americans, it elicits a far smaller increase."[84]

Perceptions of criminal activity: "White Americans overestimate the proportion of crime committed by people of color, and associate people of color with criminality. For example, white respondents in a 2010 survey overestimated the actual share of burglaries, illegal drug sales, and juvenile crime committed by African Americans by 20-30 percent. In addition, implicit bias research has uncovered widespread and deep-seated tendencies among whites—including criminal justice practitioners—to associate blacks and Latinos with criminality."[85]

Perceptions of racial discrimination: 52 percent of Blacks, 23 percent of Hispanics, 25 percent of Asians, and 5 percent of Whites say that their race has hurt their ability to get ahead. 76 percent of Blacks, 58 percent of Hispanics, 76 percent of Asians, and 33 percent of Whites say that they have faced discrimination. 60 percent of Blacks, 48 percent of Hispanics, 36 percent of Asians, and 26 percent of Whites say that people have treated them as though they thought they were not smart."[86]

Police use of force: "African Americans are far more likely than whites and other groups to be the victims of use of force by the police, even when racial disparities in crime are taken into account."[87]

Protective mothers: "This is where [White] helicoptering and black mothering diverge. While [White] helicopter moms are busy multiplying their children's privilege and advantages, many black moms are fighting to protect their children from the structural disadvantages that keep opportunity just out of reach."[88]

Public school climate and safety:

<u>Referrals to law enforcement and arrests:</u> "During the 2015–16 school year, black students represented 15 percent of the total student enrollment, and 31 percent of students who were referred to law enforcement or arrested. . . . White students represented 49 percent of the total student enrollment, and accounted for 36 percent of those referred to law enforcement or arrested."

<u>Students reported as harassed or bullied:</u> "Black students were 15 percent of overall student enrollment and 35 percent of those harassed or bullied on the basis of race. . . . White students were 49 percent of the student enrollment, 29 percent of students harassed or bullied on the basis of race."

<u>Students disciplined for harassment or bullying:</u> "Black students represented 15 percent of all students enrolled, and accounted for 22 percent of those disciplined for harassment or bullying; white students represented 49 percent of students enrolled and 45 percent of those disciplined."

<u>Students receiving one or more out-of-school suspensions, by race and sex:</u> "Black male students represented 8 percent of enrolled students and accounted for 25 percent of students who received an out-of-school suspension. Black female students represented 8 percent of the student enrollment and accounted for 14 percent of students who received an out-of-school suspension. . . . White male students represented 25 percent of students enrolled and 24 percent of students who received an out-of-school suspension. White female students represented 24 percent of students enrolled and 8 percent of students who received an out-of-school suspension."

Students receiving expulsions, by race and sex: "Black male students represented 8 percent of enrolled students and accounted for 23 percent of students expelled. Black female students represented 8 percent of the student enrollment and accounted for 10 percent of students who were expelled. . . . White male students represented 25 percent of students enrolled and 27 percent of students who were expelled. White female students represented 24 percent of students enrolled and 10 percent of students who were expelled."[89]

School funding: "School districts where the majority of students enrolled are students of color receive $23 billion less in education funding than predominantly white school districts, despite serving the same number of students—a dramatic discrepancy that underscores the depth of K-12 funding inequities in the U.S. . . . When researchers at EdBuild disregarded income levels, they found that districts serving large numbers of students of color receive, on average, 16 percent, or about $2,200, less per student than largely White districts. In 21 states, nonwhite school districts received less funding per pupil than white districts."[90]

Toxic waste: "In 1987, the United Church of Christ Commission for Racial Justice released its groundbreaking study 'Toxic Wastes and Race in the United States.' The report was significant because it found race to be the most potent variable in predicting where commercial hazardous waste facilities were located in the U.S., more powerful than household income, the value of homes and the estimated amount of hazardous waste generated by industry. Our new report, 'Toxic Wastes and Race at Twenty' [published in 2007], again signals clear evidence of racism where toxic waste sites are located and the way government responds to toxic contamination emergencies in people of color communities."[91]

"In answer to 'Which came first?', our findings show that rather than hazardous waste treatment, storage, and disposal facilities 'attracting' people of color, neighborhoods with already disproportionate and growing concentrations of people of color appear to 'attract' new facility siting."[92]

Traffic stops: "Stanford University researchers have compiled the most comprehensive evidence to date suggesting there is a pattern of racial disparities in traffic stops. . . . The traffic-stop data—the largest such dataset ever collected—points to pervasive inequality in how police decide to stop and search white and minority drivers."[93]

- "An idyllic afternoon of Little League baseball followed by pizza and Italian ice turned harrowing when two police officers in Bridgeport,

Connecticut, stopped Woodrow Vereen Jr. for driving through a yellow light.... One of the officers instructed Vereen, who is black, to get out of the car and lean over the trunk, and then patted him down. Vereen could see tears welling in the eyes of his 7- and 3-year-old sons as they peered through the rear window. He cringed as folks at a nearby bus stop watched one of the officers look through his car. He never consented to the 2015 search, which turned up nothing illegal.... Rosie Villegas-Smith, a Mexican-born U.S. citizen, who has lived in Phoenix for 28 years, has been stopped a couple of times by Maricopa County sheriff's deputies.... 'There's a power that they want to exert, that you have to experience. And what do you do about it?' Smith said. 'There's an embedded terror in our community.'"[94]

Transportation: "The United States remains a country where many forms of transportation are effectively still segregated—whites and minorities ride different kinds of transportation, resulting in an unequal ability to reach jobs, education, and a better life."[95]

Unemployment: During 2018, the unemployment rate was 3.9 percent among all races in the United States, 3.5 percent for Whites, 6.5 percent for African Americans, 3.0 percent for Asian Americans, and 4.7 percent for Hispanic Americans.[96]

Voting:

1. "Studies show . . . that voter fraud is vanishingly rare in the United States."

2. "States with a history of voting discrimination—which until 2013 had to submit changes to their election laws to the federal government for approval before going into effect—operated 868 fewer polling places on Election Day in 2016."

3. "Long lines are problematic, most notably for low-income people and people of color, who are less likely to have flexible employment and child care options that allow them to wait in line for hours at a time. A study from the Massachusetts Institute of Technology found that, on average, Hispanic voters spend one and a half times as long in line than their white counterparts. African Americans spend nearly twice as long in line to vote."

4. "In recent years, multiple states have adopted strict voter ID laws. . . . These laws place a disproportionate burden on people of color. In

Indiana, for example, one study found that white citizens were 11.5 percentage points more likely than black citizens to have the accepted credentials to vote."

5. "Purging voter rolls unduly targets people of color."[97]

Wages by gender and race: In 2018, the median weekly earnings of full-time Black women workers over sixteen was 89 percent of what full-time working Black men earned and 65.3 percent of what full-time working White men earned. Black men earned 73.4 percent of what White men earned. Hispanic women earned 85.7 percent of what Hispanic men earned and 61.6 percent of what White men earned. Hispanic men earned 72.9 percent of what White men earned. Asian women earned 75.5 percent of what Asian men earned and 93.5 percent of what White men earned. Asian men earned 23.9 percent more than what White men earned. White women earned 81.5 percent of what White men earned.[98]

Wealth: "The difference in wealth between typical households in each racial group ballooned to $236,500 in 2009, up from $85,000 in 1984, according to the study, released Wednesday [February 27, 2013]. By 2009, the median net worth of white families was $265,000, while blacks had only $28,500."[99]

"If current economic trends continue, the average black household will need 228 years to accumulate as much wealth as their white counterparts hold today. For the average Latino family, it will take 84 years. Absent significant policy interventions, or a seismic change in the American economy, people of color will never close the gap."[100]

Individual Stories

Called the N-word at a seminary: "African-American students say they matriculated to Duke Divinity School expecting to enhance their calling with top-notch theological training at a prestigious program. But instead, they say, they entered a racial nightmare seemingly from another era, with students being called the N-word and other slurs in class, consistently receiving lower grades than their white colleagues. . . . The intolerant atmosphere also targets Latino and LGBTQ students."[101]

Fear for safety: "I'm 62 and living here [in Louisiana] and now I have a fear for my safety. It's not just North Korea setting off a nuclear bomb, but

Inhabiting Every Nook and Cranny of American Life

suppose white supremacists decide to come out of the woods of Louisiana one night when I'm in church?"[102]

Followed: From a White male with a Black girlfriend: "At some point, three black boys (probably high-schoolers) were walking behind us. We didn't pay them any mind until we distinctly heard someone say, 'Yo, she darker than he is.' My girlfriend and I kind of looked at each other, trying to affirm nonverbally that we'd heard exactly what we thought we'd heard. We kept walking. Then one of them said, 'What color your baby gonna come out?' We didn't respond, didn't even look back; we just kept walking. 'Hey! I said, what color your baby gonna come out?'"[103]

Gardening while Black: "For nearly two years, a man tilled an overgrown park in a half-abandoned Detroit neighborhood into a tiny urban farm, filling the earth with the seeds of kale and spinach and radishes. He was black. For half of that time, the man, Marc Peeples, 32, was the subject of dozens of calls to the police—the allegations growing more serious with each call—by three women who lived on a street facing the park. They were white."[104]

Growing up Black: "Throughout my life, something—the kink of my hair or my 'attitude'—would mark me as inferior, worthy of ridicule, humiliation or ostracism. . . . Much to my dismay, my blackness seemed to be the salient thing about me. One of my classmates had a gift for inventing creative ways to make fun of my kinky hair, and he got enough people laughing to send me home in tears for a good part of my freshman and sophomore years of high school."[105]

Nasty teasing: "I'm Hmong-American. My siblings—my younger sister, my older sister and my little brother—we made up basically the Asian student body. . . . When we're walking they [other students] would slant their eyes and say, 'Can you see? Can you see?' You know, you're supposed to go to school and you're supposed to feel safe and I didn't feel safe. I felt tormented."[106]

Pushed toward the edge of a subway platform: A Chinese American who is a registered nurse in New York City was approached by a man on a subway platform and told to go back to his own country. The man kept coming closer and closer to the Chinese American, who was forced to step toward the edge of the platform. A bystander intervened, but when the train arrived, the aggressor sat right across from the Chinese American and glared at him the entire ride, mouthing, "I'm watching you."[107]

The Uneasy Conscience of a White Christian

Slave for sale and pictures of a noose: "An unwanted spotlight is on Naperville [Illinois] schools after a student was accused of making a racist Craigslist ad last month that featured a picture of a black student with the title 'slave for sale.'" On Snapchat, an eighth-grade student was sent the message, "Yo, you just need to kill yourself," plus pictures of a noose and of the KKK.[108]

To me, these statistics and stories demonstrate the wide extent of racism in the United States. Others, however, believe that poverty and social class explain racial disparities just as well. To say that racism is the cause of the disparities is to jump to a conclusion faster than the evidence warrants, they say.

To this I reply that, yes, poverty and social class are undoubtedly involved in some of the racial disparities. But that does not entail that race is not also involved, for a number of reasons. First, the sheer quantity of the racial disparities makes it unlikely that poverty and social class are the *only* explanation of *every single* racial disparity. Second, some of the statistics involve studies in which poverty and class cannot possibly be involved, as poverty and class played no role in the racial discrimination. These studies include the one involving names, the one involving medical algorithms, and the one involving traffic stops. Third, there have been racially discriminatory policies, and racially injurious actions directed to individuals, that affect both poor and wealthy people of color, such as redlining and White homeowners driving out wealthy Black people who have moved into their White neighborhoods. Fourth, the history of racism in the United States is a background condition that must be considered. If it is, it makes it much more likely, again, that poverty and social class are not the only explanation of racial disparities. Fifth, the high quantity of stories involving racially injurious behavior toward individuals, only a very small percentage of which are mentioned above, lends support, still again, to the assertion that poverty and social class are not likely to be the only explanations of the racial disparities.

A last reply is that poverty and social class might themselves be largely a result of racism. Someone who invokes them to explain racial disparities must present solid evidence for believing that they are not the result of racism. In fact, however, there is good evidence to think that they are. This evidence appeals to racially injurious policies that directly contribute to poverty, such as job discrimination and bank loan discrimination.

Inhabiting Every Nook and Cranny of American Life

One is, accordingly, justified in saying that there are a number of takeaways from these statistics and stories. The first is that racism in the United States is not limited to the highly publicized events that are reported in the media. It extends to a wide array of significant domains, to put it modestly, and to every detail of American life, to put it more accurately. This means, second, that the United States is highly racialized. Race is a difference that makes a difference, often a big one. Third, the extent of the disparities makes one wonder whether there is any "place called 'innocence'"[109] in which White Americans are free from complicity or association with racial disparities. Fourth, racial harmony does not just involve harmonious relationships among individuals, such as having friends with someone from a different race or a White person attending a non-White church. Harmony also involves undoing the racial disparities in groups, corporate entities, and governments. Fifth, White concern with racism should not be only with the Whiteness of individual White people. It must also be with these groups, corporate entities, and governments. Sixth, a high percentage of the racial disparities involve social forces over which people of color have no control. Individual choices and Black-on-Black crime cannot explain these disparities. Seventh, a change of moral character in White individuals, though necessary, is not sufficient to bring about harmony between White folks and non-White folks. The disparities listed must also be addressed. And, last, the extent of these disparities explains why Saidiya Hartman, a Columbia University professor of English and comparative literature asks, "Did slavery ever really end?"[110]

The effect of reading these statistics and stories should be the realization that the United States still has a serious racism problem. One cannot legitimately believe that people of color and White people have equal opportunities just because federal law prohibits racial discrimination. The sheer extent of the statistics and stories entails that dealing with the US race problem should be a high priority for both individuals and corporate entities.

8

Is Abortion Worse than Racism?

RECENTLY A BLACK ACQUAINTANCE was trying to convince a White person that racism is an important issue. The White person said, "Abortion is this important," holding his hand at eye level, "and racism is this important," holding his other hand a foot lower.

Both were students at an evangelical Christian college. Their encounter is representative of a major difference between White evangelicals (and conservative Catholics), who typically regard abortion as worse than racism, and Black Christians, who generally regard racism as at least as wrong as abortion.

Some Christians respond to the White evangelical view by downplaying the wrongness of abortion. I, however, concur with White evangelicals that abortion is a serious moral wrong but also believe that racism is just as seriously wrong. Eliminating racism is at least as important as eliminating abortion for three reasons: racism produces deaths, the decreased quality of life experienced by recipients of racism is highly injurious, and the harm to oneself of racially biased attitudes is severe.

If these reasons are sound, then those who elevate the wrongness of abortion over the wrongness of racism should change so as to advocate against racism just as strongly as they do against abortion. I shall not say anything about abortion itself, about whether there are extenuating circumstances that might justify some abortions. My sole concern is with whether anti-abortionists, who believe that abortion is gravely wrong, should also believe that racism is gravely wrong.

Death

Those who believe that abortion is worse than racism almost certainly do so because they believe that abortion is a life-and-death issue, whereas racism is not. Abortion, they typically say, is the killing of a person. And persons are made in God's image, which means that they have the highest value among all of God's creatures. Killing them is the highest affront to God. So we should be much more concerned about abortion than racism, the argument concludes.[111]

The correct response to this argument is to say that racism also kills. It did in the past—during slavery times, Reconstruction, and the lynching era—and it does so now. The statistics I presented in chapter 7 on racial disparities show that Black people die at higher rates in a number of domains than do White people, including higher execution rates, infant deaths, deaths of new mothers, police killings, and general life expectancy.

Two considerations show that racism is involved in these deaths—a general fact and studies that deal with the role of race in health care. The general fact is that the death disparities are spread over several domains, not just one—police encounters, capital punishment, maternal deaths, and infant deaths. This general fact is significant. If there were just one particular way in which a death disparity exists—just one way in the entire United States—and if there were not a history of racism in the United States, we might wonder what causes the disparity. But as there are a number of domains in which death disparities exist, and as the United States has a long history of racism, we are justified in believing that racism plays a large part in producing current disparities.

This general consideration is reinforced significantly by several dozen other disparities that link race to a lower quality of life, some of which are cited in chapter 7. When these other disparities are set in the context of the history of racism in the United States, it becomes very highly probable, almost certain, that racism is involved in them, and by implication, also in the death disparities.

This conclusion is reinforced by studies that specifically show the impact of race on health care. Here are several, summarized from chapter 7:

The Uneasy Conscience of a White Christian

- "The evidence is strong that it is the chronic effect of the stress of racism . . . that takes its toll on pregnancy, childbirth, and care for a newborn after birth."[112]
- Poverty alone does not "account for the fact that black people are sicker and have shorter life spans than their white complements."[113]
- "An algorithm widely used in US hospitals to allocate health care to patients has been systematically discriminating against black people, a sweeping analysis has found."[114]

If these studies showing the involvement of racism in health care are valid, the implication is that racism is very probably also operative with police, judges, and juries who are responsible for the deaths of Black Americans. This extension to the criminal justice system is further supported by the general fact that police, judges, and juries often are among those who are socialized to believe that Black Americans are more likely to be criminals than are White Americans. This fact in turn affects police behavior toward Black Americans and jury deliberation in capital crimes involving Black Americans, especially because it has been shown in a study by the Equal Justice Initiative that jury selection in the United States is racially discriminatory.[115]

The advocate of the greater wrongness of abortion compared to racism might respond by saying that there are vastly more deaths in the United States due to abortion than are due to racism—619,591 abortions in 2018 alone, according to the Centers for Disease Control.[116] This makes abortion a much more important issue than racism, the advocate would infer.

The correct reply is to admit that there are, indeed, many more abortions than deaths caused by racism, but that this is not decisive in judging the moral importance of eliminating deaths due to racism. Between 1877 and 1950, there were "only" 4,084 racial terror lynchings in twelve Southern states, according to Equal Justice Initiative.[117] Yet lynchings are commonly thought to be morally horrific, especially because many Christians were involved in them.[118]

Those who believe that abortion is worse than racism might also reply by saying that abortion is intentional, whereas current racism that leads to death is rarely intentional, as it was for lynching and mass killings in an earlier era. This fact means, they say, that abortion is worse than racist acts that come from unconscious bias, because the law typically distinguishes between first-degree murder, which is intentional, and involuntary manslaughter, which is not. The former is given a more severe penalty than the latter because it is worse than the latter.

I do not want to get into the issue of whether death due to abortion is intentional, but want to say simply that even if those who believe that abortion is worse than racism are right in describing abortion as "intentional killing," that still would not show that abortion is worse than racism. For it is the overall harm done by racism that makes it morally on a level with abortion, not just the intention. The numerous deaths and injuries that have resulted from not having seat belts or airbags in cars were certainly unintended, but the fact that there have been any such deaths is seriously harmful. The lack of intention to harm does not mitigate the seriousness of the actual harm. In the same way, the fact that actions derived from unconscious racial bias produce deaths does not mitigate the harmfulness of those actions. There should be no deaths that are produced by racial bias, unconscious or not.

Lower Quality of Life

A second component of the overall case for regarding racism to be as wrong as abortion is that it affects the quality of life of its recipients in a number of significant ways. These ways have been documented by numerous, reliable statistical studies, only some of which are cited in chapter 7. These statistics show that well-known incidents of racial harm are not just isolated aberrations in an otherwise nonracist society. We live in a more thoroughly racist society than most White Americans are aware of, and the harm of racism is both widespread and intense.

This last point is of utmost importance—the harm of racism reaches into nearly every area of the lives of people of color, and in many of these areas it is highly injurious. When one comes to appreciate these two facts, one must come to believe that racism is seriously wrong—harming people in highly injurious ways often prevents them from having intrinsically good experiences, to put it in philosophical terms, or to experience an abundant life, to put it in Jesus's words (John 10:10). And that is an affront to God, because people are image-bearers of God who are made to have an abundance of intrinsically good experiences.

Moreover, the Golden Rule is relevant to this quality-of-life consideration. It requires that we imagine we are the others mentioned in the Golden Rule and then imagine we are the recipient of something harmful done to us. Doing this two-step imagining is a way of getting us to recognize what is right and wrong, and it is also a way of getting us to discern the degree of rightness and wrongness of certain actions. We can feel *that* something is wrong, and we can feel *how* wrong it is. My claim here is that when those of us who are White do this two-step imagining, we will perceive that the harms that people of color currently experience are severely wrong.

Besides the numerous ways in which racial harm affects people of color cited in chapter 7, a good share of the harm caused by racism is emotional. Here are some of the toxic emotions that racism can cause:

- *Fear*: News of police shootings and the use of excessive force by police, White on Black, can engender fear of being another victim. It can also engender a general distrust of the police. White people can readily believe that local police "serve and protect," but many people of color believe that police are not to be trusted to do these.

- *Alienation*: One racial microaggression or incident probably will not make the recipient feel alienated, but numerous ones can easily do so. See chapter 9 for "Caroline's" account of how this happened to her.

- *Rejection*: Alienation is the sense of being other—I am not part of the dominant culture in the United States. Alienation can produce rejection. Recipients of constant racialisms can feel as though they are rejected by people in the dominant culture. Recall AJ's statement in the introduction that he feels that America does not like him.

- *Having less worth*: Alienation and rejection can easily lead to the sense that one has less worth. The slogans "Black is beautiful" and "Black lives matter" clearly are ways to respond to this sense.

- *Hopelessness and meaninglessness*: It is not hard to see how these four feelings can lead to a sense of hopelessness and meaninglessness. In his *Race Matters*, Cornel West states that nihilism pervades Black communities. By "nihilism" he means "the lived experience of coping with a life of horrifying meaninglessness, hopelessness, and (most important) lovelessness."[119]

No doubt some people of color have not experienced these emotions as a result of racial disparities or incidents. Still, a significant number have experienced one or more of them. Their stories are scattered about the Internet and in books and articles.

Is Abortion Worse than Racism?

Harm to Oneself

The distinction between explicit, mean-spirited racism and unconscious, prereflective racism is vital for the claim that racism is at least as bad as abortion. Most Americans rightly disavow mean-spirited racism. But if what I have said in chapter 2 about racial socialization is correct, most of us White Americans have a sense of racial superiority that is submerged in the deep parts of our character. The key to accepting this claim lies in realizing that a sense of racial superiority can work its way into people even if they are not consciously hateful and mean-spirited. If advocates of the claim that abortion is worse than racism were to come to this realization, they would become alarmed at the fact that they themselves, along with many others, might have a hidden sense of racial superiority. They would see that racism needs to be taken as seriously as abortion.

This sense of racial superiority, whether overt or hidden, undermines one's central Christian identity. It does so because humility is central to one's Christian identity, and the sense of racial superiority is exactly the opposite of humility. If George Yancy is right in saying that the sense of racial superiority in White people is a central and pervasive feature of one's character, a structuring orientation (see chapter 2), then to have a sense of racial superiority is for pride to be a central and pervasive feature of one's character. It is not just a one-time or occasional failing, but a worm at the core of one's identity.

Racial pride, whether mean-spirited or prereflective, also leads to other sins, obstructs cross-racial relationships with other people, and impairs one's relationship to God.

Racial pride leads to racially injurious behavior because it undermines sensitivity to the racial consequences of what one does. It does this because one who has racial pride does not value people of different races as much as one values people of one's own race. If one were to regard people of other races as having the same value as people of one's own race, one would be sensitive to the racial consequences of one's actions. But if one regards one's own race as superior to other races, even if as a submerged part of one's character, one's attentiveness to the racial consequences of one's actions toward people of color is impaired. One does not value those consequences as much as one values the consequences of what one does to people of one's own race.

Racial pride also interferes with cross-racial friendships. It does this because true friendships require that each friend fully value the other.

Without this equality, the friendship cannot continue. Indeed, it cannot truly begin. This point is connected to the belief that all are made in the image of God. The sense of racial superiority undermines this belief. It does so because the belief that humans are made in God's image is an egalitarian belief. It entails that all are equal from God's perspective. So if one has a sense of racial superiority, one believes that people of other races are not fully made in God's image. They are less than human. It is hard to imagine a friendship in which one of the friends believes the other to be less than human. Southern slaveholders may have thought they were friends with some of their slaves, but they were tragically mistaken.

There is more. Racial pride obstructs one's relationship to God in the way described in chapter 3. One cannot take in God's grace if one has a sense of racial superiority. This sense of superiority is something about which one can boast to oneself: "I am something because I am White. I am better than those others who are not White"—a boasting that is likely to be a submerged stance that colors all one's feelings, attitudes, and ways of thinking about people of different races. Accepting God's freely given saving grace, which is essential to one's Christian identity, cannot coexist with this self-boasting. One could *say* that one has accepted God's saving grace, but that declaration would be undercut by a sense of racial superiority. This possibility raises serious concern for the one who regards abortion as worse than racism.

Together, the three considerations I have described show that racism needs to be taken as seriously as anti-abortionists take abortion to be: racism kills, it reduces the quality of life of people of color in a wide variety of serious ways, and it gravely harms the one who has racially injurious feelings, attitudes, and ways of thinking. The conclusion is that anti-abortionists should also be anti-racist just as strongly as they are anti-abortionist.

Israel

Racial Undertones

Israel was forty when we talked. He lives in Florida.

BOTH MY MOTHER AND father were born in Puerto Rico. They were raised there until they were young teenagers, when they came to New York. I was born in New York and grew up in Chicago.

I identify as Latino. On forms, I put down Hispanic if I have to. But I prefer Latino, because Hispanic is a catchall term that generalizes different groups of people based on the fact that they all speak Spanish, and it doesn't account for where they come from. My people are from Latin America—Puerto Rico—as opposed to Spain. I knew I was Puerto Rican as a child, but it wasn't something I thought of as racialized. I knew there were Black people, Brown people, and White people, but I didn't pay much attention to that.

The first time I had a racialized experience was in sixth grade. We had moved to the northwest side of Chicago, at the very edge of the city, just before you start to hit the suburbs. The neighborhood we lived in had mostly Greeks, Italians, and some Polish people, all of whom I considered to be White. Not long after we met, a couple of White kids in the neighborhood started using words like "spick" and "beaner" when talking to me. They said, "Hey, spick," or "Hey, beaner." And they teased and made jokes about me using those words.

The Uneasy Conscience of a White Christian

I had never heard the words before and didn't know what they meant. I picked up, though, that they had something to do with my being Puerto Rican, as I was the only Latino in the group of kids I was a part of. I remember thinking, "Okay, I'm part of this group, and I know that some of the teasing and joking I'm getting is because I'm new and by far the youngest. But it also feels that there is something extra going on that is clearly happening because I'm Puerto Rican. And I don't like it. It doesn't feel good at all."

At times, I felt isolated and hurt. I lost out in the jockeying for position within the group when we played games or did something. Although I was part of the group, I never felt that I fully belonged to it. I asked myself, "What is this about?" I was not being ostracized, but for the first time in my life I found myself wondering how much my race had to do with how I was being treated. It got to the point that I made the decision to keep the others at arm's distance. For the most part, we were friends, because the teasing and joking were never everyday occurrences. However, I was always very guarded with the group.

"Spick" and "beaner" are clearly racist words. But, while they hurt, I never felt that they were directed at me with hate or vitriol. It was not malicious, overt racism I experienced, such as, "You're a stupid spick. Why are you in our neighborhood? Get out of here!" It felt more like racialized teasing and joking.

Now as an adult I have come to learn that this type of targeted discrimination is called "interpersonal discrimination." Unlike more overt forms of racism and discrimination, it consists of behaviors that often occur in much more nuanced and subtle ways during negative nonverbal, paraverbal, and verbal social interactions. Often this type of racial humor, or these types of racial utterances, like the ones I've described, can easily be dismissed as no big deal or as simple rudeness. However, these interactions are characterized by their racial undertones. And while the impact they can have is different for everyone, research has shown that their impact on an individual has the potential to be very significant. For me, personally, these interactions were, indeed, significant in my life, so much so that even now I still am learning exactly to what extent.

That said, I'm confident that no one in the group I was part of would not have thought they were engaging in any form of racial discrimination. And they certainly would not have considered themselves or anyone in the group a racist. Still, the interpersonal discrimination occurred. Maybe it was due to racial ignorance. At the very least, it was racially insensitive. Certainly it was to me.

Most of the kids in my group didn't participate in the interpersonal discrimination. However, most in the group heard it occur, as well as some other overtly racist comments made in the group. But they all chose to remain silent about it and never addressed it when it occurred or with me directly.

I definitely heard overt racism in the neighborhood on occasion as well. It was never directed at me, but it occurred in a more general way. Our neighborhood had brick bungalows, and we all often sat on the front steps of them, talking. During one of these times, the conversation drifted to the possibility of Black people moving into our predominantly White neighborhood, and one of the older guys from the neighborhood, whose steps we often sat on, said, "Well, you know what happens when Black people move into a neighborhood. It brings the property values down. That happens. It's a real thing." Someone else said that it was because of the way Black people acted.

I was the only Latino there, still in junior high, feeling too alone, too young, and too intimidated to say anything to a grown man I didn't know well in front of a group of people who did know him yet had said nothing. I said to myself, "That's clearly racist. Do the rest of you actually agree with that garbage?!" I thought, "What do you really feel about us as a Latino family being in the neighborhood? Even though you act like you're cool with us, are you really cool with us? What have you said about us Latinos moving into the neighborhood?"

Despite the negative racialized experiences, living in that neighborhood overall was pretty positive. What is clear to me, though, is that if I had been Black, or had been a much darker-skinned Latino, I very likely would have had far more negative racialized experiences and perhaps would have been the recipient of much more of the overt type of directly targeted racism.

In one way, my racial experiences growing up were unique. For most of my childhood, I did not live in a Latino neighborhood, and I did not hang out only with Latinos. My friend group has always been diverse. The first neighborhood my family lived in was mixed, with Mexicans, Indians, Whites, and Puerto Ricans. And although the neighborhood we later moved to was predominantly White, with no other Latinos, the grade school there was very diverse. It bused in students from the west and south sides of Chicago. The high school I went to in the mid 1990s had balanced percentages of Latinos, Blacks, Whites, and Asians. The whole school was pretty proud of this. We even had a week-long event called International Days when the different cultures in the school were celebrated.

There were many more Black guys than Latinos on the football teams I was on in high school and college, and so I often hung out with Black guys. After college, both in Illinois and southern Florida, I have worked closely with, and built strong, close friendships with, people from different races and cultures through my work and outside of it as well. I have been fully a part of an all-Latino Pentecostal church, a majority-White nondenominational Bible church, a mixed-race Christian and Missionary Alliance church, and a very multicultural Southern Baptist church. I have also been to all-Black Gospel churches, mixed-race charismatic churches, and all-Mexican churches in Mexico. In these diverse settings and relationships, I intentionally immersed myself in the families, cultures, and faith experiences I interacted with. In so doing, I learned a great deal.

These diverse experiences have impacted who I have become and how I live my life. One of the most significant impacts they have had on me is that they have made me comfortable in many different racial settings. Because of these experiences and others, God has given me the ability to more naturally and authentically join and serve many different communities for the sake of sharing and proclaiming the saving truth about the unfailing love of Jesus, our Lord. I value the diverse ways of worshipping him, and I am blessed that because of my experiences I can genuinely and comfortably worship God in different cultural settings. I don't feel that I'm not being my normal self during these times. I'm just being my authentic self as a part of the communities in those settings.

9

"But I Didn't Mean to Hurt You"
Racial Microaggressions and Whiteness

RACISM IN THE UNITED States is widely thought to be overt and explicit, such as what White nationalists or members of the Ku Klux Klan do or say. Their avowed declarations are consciously directed at Black, Brown, or Jewish people and are clearly identifiable as hateful attacks.

There are other negative racial expressions, however, that are not overt or explicitly racist, often not thought to be negative by those who make them, and not motivated by hate. Nevertheless, they have negative effects on their recipients. These expressions are called "microaggressions."

Columbia University psychologist Derald Wing Sue describes racial microaggressions as "the brief and everyday slights, insults, indignities and denigrating messages sent to people of color by well-intentioned white people who are unaware of the hidden messages being communicated."[120] These communications, he says, "are usually outside the level of conscious awareness of perpetrators."[121] People whose communications convey a slight, insult, or indignity do not mean to hurt the recipient. Their intentions are not hateful, denigrating, or belittling.

I had not heard of microaggressions before preparing the course on race and justice at Wheaton College. When I did learn of them, I wondered whether Derald Wing Sue's assertion about the extent of microaggressions was true in the Christian context I inhabited. He writes: "Studies support the fact that people of color frequently experience microaggressions, that it is a continuing reality in their day-to-day interactions with friends, neighbors, co-workers, teachers, and employers in academic, social and public settings."[122] He also states that "studies reveal that racial microaggressions have powerful detrimental consequences to people of color. They are often made to feel excluded, untrustworthy, second-class citizens, and abnormal."[123]

I decided to ask students of color at Wheaton College whether they had been the recipient of racial microaggressions from other students and, if so, what they were. I got long lists. I also got their reactions to the microaggressions, which often were deeply expressive, describing hurt, frustration, and anger. I got the same lists and reactions from former students at Trinity College in Deerfield, Illinois, another Christian college where I had taught for thirty-one years before teaching at Wheaton College. The lists and reactions described below come from twenty-five students and former students, sixteen during the 2017–2018 academic year at Wheaton College, and nine former students at Trinity College.

Though the racial microaggressions described by the former students from Trinity College occurred some years ago, they are not out of date, as people of color continue to experience microaggressions. As "Dawn" stated in 2019, "I am worried that in the present state of our country the subtle insults I continue to receive will become more pointed."

I was able to get these lists and reactions because the students of color at these colleges knew me, a White professor, to be someone they could trust to handle what they said with care and respect. Even though the lists are extensive, one cannot infer that these two colleges are worse than other Christian colleges and universities or worse than nonreligious colleges and universities. I ask readers to suspend judgment about such comparisons.

What can be said, though, in the words of one of the students I talked to, is that "Christians who are well-meaning still have implicit biases that they don't know exist and that shape the way they interact with others." It is highly likely that what is true of Christians at these two Christian colleges is also true of Christians elsewhere in the United States, whether in college or not.

It might be thought that students of color at these colleges found them hard places to be at because of the quantity and variety of microaggressions they were recipients of. Though this was true to varying degrees, it was also true that at least some students of color were devoted to the college they were at or had attended.

"But I Didn't Mean to Hurt You"

"Kyler's" response to my question about whether he liked being at Wheaton College is typical of the sentiments of the students of color I talked to at Wheaton College: "I love Wheaton College. I want people to know about microaggressions, because I care about Wheaton." "Micah" went through a lot of depression while at Trinity College, but declared, "I definitely appreciated my time at Trinity."

These are my sentiments as well about both colleges. This article is not intended to cast a negative light on these colleges, but simply to make visible a prominent reality in the lives of people of color so that those who are uninformed about it, like I once was, can become sensitive to it.

What Makes a Microaggression an Aggression?

It may seem too strong to characterize a message that is not intended to be denigrating as an "aggression." This is certainly true from the perspective of one who unintentionally sends the message. But from the perspective of one who receives the message, "aggression" is not too strong.

Consider this scenario: You, a non-Asian person, ask a new Asian-looking acquaintance where they are from. They mention a town and state in the United States. You then ask, "Where are you really from?" or "What country are you from?" You are asking only out of curiosity, perhaps even loving curiosity, as you want to get to know your acquaintance better. But the person who fields your question hears a subtext: "You are not willing to accept my answer. You are stereotyping me. You would not ask this question of a new acquaintance of your own color, so why are you asking it of me?" From this perspective, the question causes the Asian recipient to feel other than you. It feels insensitive and unfeeling, somewhat aggressive. After being asked the question by a number of different people, the recipient begins to feel alienated.

People who are recipients of microaggressions experience them not just once or twice, but numerous times, and not just the same one, but a variety of them. The questions or statements may feel innocent the first few times, but eventually they feel abrasive because of their sheer quantity.

This happened to "Caroline," who has an Asian ancestry, and who was not bothered by the questions and comments about her identity when she first arrived at college. Later, though, she became bothered by them: "Microaggressions have a way of starting out seemingly small and innocent, but over time they transform into harmful and potentially dangerous wounds in the already difficult life of a minority person." Caroline continues, "After a while, they began to wear me down and infect me with a negativity I did not previously have. I began to feel defensive and constantly on the lookout for further attacks."

Notice the strong words that Caroline uses to describe the process. Though at first she regarded what was said as small and innocent, as time passed she began to feel worn down and defensive. As more time passed, what was said to her came to feel like attacks. During this process, she became more and more fearful of further comments that would injure her.

Although some microaggressions seem innocent, others are not so innocent. A White person touching the hair of a Black person, female or male, is not so innocent, and so is a White person *asking* to touch a Black person's hair. In White US culture, it is almost always off limits for one White person to touch the hair of another White person out of curiosity, whether or not one asks to do so, even if the other person is a close friend. The same limits apply across races, no matter the race.

White people, to be sure, are curious about Black hair and want to know what it feels like. But curiosity has limits. There are questions that are intrusive and that may make the other person feel violated or disrespected. Asking what another person's hair feels like is such a question.

Part of what prompts microaggressions directed at people of color is "differentism": treating people who are different with unwarranted attention or curiosity, thinking of them as odd, as not like oneself, such as staring at someone who is extremely tall or being intrusively curious about someone who has a mohawk haircut.

Racial differences prompt such attention and curiosity. But racial microaggressions often have an added component: a sense of superiority or normalcy. Here "normalcy" is not just a descriptive word referring to the amount of people in a given social group, but a value word carrying the idea that those who are in the majority are better than those who are not.

Although being the recipient of repeated comments based only on being different may seem harmless, it can still have the same effect as being the recipient of comments based on a sense of superiority. Those derived from a sense of superiority, of course, convey, even if unintended, that the recipient is inferior.

Although Black people and other people of color are recipients of some common microaggressions, there are differences. So I will list the microaggressions separately. The categories are Black, Hispanic, and Asian.

People in other categories, including Native American and Middle Eastern, plus those who are mixtures of two or more categories, are also recipients of microaggressions, which often have the same underlying tone of otherness and exclusion that Black, Hispanic, and Asian people experience. Those who are mixed get additional comments that intensify their feeling of not fully belonging to just one category—not fully Black, Hispanic, Asian, or White—and thus not fully belonging anywhere.

Some of the students I contacted reported that the microaggressions they experienced came only from White people, but others reported that, though the majority of microaggressions came from White people, some also came from other people of color.

Microaggressions Directed to Black Students

Here is a list of microaggressions experienced by Black students from other students at the same college.

1. Asking to feel my hair
2. Touching my hair without asking
3. Saying that my hair is different and looks funny
4. "Oh!! Your hair looks like a rat in the trash can!"
5. Assuming that I only listen to rap music
6. Assuming that I live in the inner city
7. Assuming that my mom and family aren't Christian because I was born outside of wedlock
8. Assuming I'm angry when I express passion about something
9. Commenting on the way I speak
10. Telling me that I speak incorrect English when I am speaking in Ebonics (AAVE)
11. Being called on to explain the history of an African American spiritual
12. Assuming that I know the names of hip-hop songs
13. Asking whether I am at college for football or basketball
14. Asking whether my scholarship is for diversity or assuming that my scholarship was given to me solely because I am Black

15. Asking me to freestyle
16. "Wow! That's so great you live with both of your parents."
17. "I love hanging out with you so much that sometimes I forget you're not White."
18. "You're the Whitest Black girl I know."
19. "Let's not make them [White people] feel uncomfortable here."
20. "Black babies are cuter than normal babies."
21. "What's up, my nigga?"
22. Having the issue of race dismissed by students during class discussions
23. Being asked by other students in a group project to do the smallest task in the project
24. Being asked by other students in a group project whether I am smart and have a good work ethic.
25. Getting peculiar glances from people who do not know me as I walk around campus, as if I do not belong at this college
26. Changing the tone or pronunciation of words to match the Black vernacular when speaking to me
27. Being told that when I and my Black friends eat meals together and walk around campus together we are intimidating to White students and give off vibes of gang activity to them
28. Having two White females run away from me when they saw me walking across campus, as if I was a threat
29. In my Race and Ethnic Relations class, White students stated that Black people should be grateful that White people brought them to America
30. While eating applesauce in the dining hall, a White male student walked up to the table I was sitting at and asked, "Black people eat applesauce?," then said, "I knew Black people ate watermelons but didn't know Black people ate applesauce," and then, "What? I can't ask you that type of question?" after I stared back at him.
31. "I have a Black friend."
32. "I know Black people who don't do that or wouldn't feel that way."
33. "Why are your people so unmotivated?"

34. "All Black people have a dystopian view and are hopeless."
35. "Why do all Black people like lemonade?" "Why do all Black people like chicken?"
36. "Hey, dog! What up?" "Hey, man!" "Yo! What up, my brother?"
37. The texture of my hair is finer than that of other Black people: "Oh, you must not be fully Black. You have to be mixed with something for your hair to be that way."
38. "You're not that dark. What are you mixed with?"
39. Calling Black people "colored": "He was a great colored boy."
40. From a faculty member: "Y'know, some people just aren't cut out for academic things. Maybe you should go home and take up a trade."

Off campus, Black students experienced these:

1. Hearing car doors being locked
2. Seeing people cross streets
3. Seeing women clutch purses
4. Being called an "Oreo"
5. Having White teenagers ask whether I sell drugs
6. Making fun of Black people's fear of police officers
7. Being followed when I go into a store
8. An offensive giggle, then, "I didn't expect that" and "It's something most Black people don't necessarily like" when I say that I enjoy country music.
9. Saying the N-word when quoting song lyrics

This last one needs a little explaining. It refers to a White person quoting the lyrics of a song performed by a Black musician. The N-word is uttered by a White person on the grounds that if a Black person can use it in a song, so can a White person—that is, not explicitly in everyday conversation as a racial slur, but in singing the song, or in repeating the phrase from the song. The idea behind the fact that using the N-word from a song is a microaggression is that the right to use the N-word does not apply to a White person as it does to a Black person, because, as Ta-Nehisi Coates points out, the context of the use of the word has changed significantly.[124]

The Uneasy Conscience of a White Christian

When "Deana" heard "Black babies are cuter than normal babies" (#20), she picked up on the word "normal" and heard the speaker intimating that Black babies are not "normal"—they are other. The statement made it clear to her that she was not part of the norm.

It was embarrassing for Deana to be asked to explain the history of an African American spiritual (#11), because she did not know that history. She felt ashamed because she thought the other people in the class thought she was dumb for not knowing her people's history. She was the only Black person in the class, so she felt it put unfair pressure on her to represent her whole race.

Something that has hurt Deana deeply over the course of her life is being called an "Oreo" (#4 in the second list). Deana's skin color is somewhere between dark brown and "white." So whenever she has been called an Oreo, she has had an identity crisis: she doesn't feel entirely Black, but she obviously is not White. Those who have called her an Oreo—both White people and other people of color—have meant it as a compliment. But to her it is one of the deepest insults someone can give, because it presupposes the superiority of being White.[125]

Kyler was startled, angry, and extremely uncomfortable when a fellow student addressed him using the N-word (#21). Although the student later apologized, Kyler was still very uncomfortable being around that student. Whenever he was asked whether he plays football (#13), which happened often, Kyler felt as though the asker thought that the only reason he was at college was to play a sport and not for his academic credentials.

One of the persons who had often been asked whether he plays football writes, "The notion that a Black man with healthy genes can't possibly attend a rigorous academic institution without being on an athletic scholarship is a form of racism." One of the students who has received a number of comments about his receiving a scholarship only because he is Black (#14) writes, "The obvious insinuation is that I don't belong at college or don't deserve my scholarship, which happens to be a National Merit Scholarship. The idea that Black students, no matter their accolades or accomplishments, are inferior to White students alienates students of color."

Brandon has been the recipient of numerous microaggressions. "They upset me when I first heard them and made me feel offended," he wrote. "However, that soon transitioned to feeling shame, because I wasn't sure I would ever be able to feel grace toward the person who had said things to me. Sometimes I wanted to remain in righteous anger, lamenting what happened, and sometimes I moved to grace so quickly that I didn't get to lament and be angry."

Because of her negative experiences, especially being told that she and her friends were intimidating when they walked together (#27), "Dawn" transferred to another college after her freshman year, but returned second semester of her sophomore year, though with great hesitancy. The negative experiences left her "hurt, a bit angry, terribly sad, and sometimes anxious."

One of the Black students reported that he had experienced the same racial stereotypes at another Christian college in the East. In both places, he felt singled out, targeted, and judged. It felt to him as though Black Americans and White Americans inhabit two different worlds.

Sometimes the pain of being the recipient of racial aggressions lasts for years. "Jasmine" experienced "endless lashings of racial injustice" while at college. As she was writing to me about those experiences, she was "second guessing whether my feelings were valid. That is how deep the wounds from the abuse are." In addition to the experiences she described to me, "there were countless other stories that replay in my mind like a recording that plays without my consent. All these experiences still make me feel angry, small, purposeless, and downright hurt." "Micah" stated that the racial microaggressions he experienced were "hard to get over. And I still feel like I am battling them in some ways eight years later."

Because of what "Moriah" experienced at college, she wanted to transfer after two years, but her mother convinced her to stay, "because that is the way the world would be anyway and there was no hiding from it. I got a thick skin from being there, which prepared me for being an adult."

Microaggressions Directed to Hispanic Students

It is sometimes thought that only Black people are the recipients of racialized comments. But this is not true. All people of color are subject to differentism and racial microaggressions. Here is a list experienced by Hispanic students from other students:

1. "It's nice that you live with both parents."
2. "Does your dad live at home?"
3. "At home do you and your family speak English?"
4. "Are you Mexican?"

5. Assuming I speak Spanish
6. Speaking Spanish to me even though we have never met
7. Assuming I "Latin dance"
8. Expecting me to know how to dance
9. Assuming I play soccer
10. Trying to pronounce my name with a "Spanish" accent
11. Asking me to say something in Spanish
12. Telling me my Spanish sounds sexy or amazing
13. Asking me to make rice and beans or to cook another Latino dish
14. Asking me whether I dream in Spanish
15. "Are you adopted?"
16. Asking why I like spicy food
17. Not being acknowledged by a new arrival when in a group of White students
18. Being asked several times whether I understood lab instructions
19. Being pushed to say where I am "really" from

"Trevor" writes, "The microaggressions I have received make me feel devalued and cause me to question my culture. The perception of others has a huge impact on how I perceive my culture, so when one questions or threatens that, it can be very problematic. I get angry."

"Alicia" says, "I felt anger and disliked when these microaggressions occurred. Right now, though, I am in a different place and can brush them off."

Microaggressions Directed to Asian Students

The following list has been experienced by Asian students from other students:

1. "Are you adopted?"
2. "Where are you really from?"
3. "Are you taking Chinese?"
4. "Do you eat rice all the time here at school too?"

5. "What kind of Asian are you?"
6. "Are you a math major?"
7. "Are you in the Music Conservatory?"
8. "Is English your first language?"
9. "This is how we do that in America."
10. "Your eyes are big for a Chinese person."
11. "You're Asian? Makes sense that you're smart."
12. "You're half Indian? So you like curry?"
13. When dating White men: "I really like you, but my parents can't know" or "We can date, but it can't be serious."
14. Being accused of stealing when I was the only person of color in my dorm suite.

Off campus, Asian students experienced these:

1. "Asian babies are not cute like White babies."
2. "You don't dress Asian."
3. "Mixed people are so unique; that is what makes them pretty." Or, "I just don't like Asian people that way."
4. Asking whether I know some person in Japan when someone finds out that I am part Japanese
5. Speaking to me in Chinese or Korean without asking whether I speak either of those languages
6. Bowing in interactions with me based on the assumption that I am Asian and not Asian American
7. Expressing annoyance about a non-Asian person squinting in a picture by saying that person "looks Asian"
8. "I know an Asian woman who looks just like you."

Caroline writes about the "Where are you from?" question (#2), which, she says, is really asking what race or ethnicity one is: "I have found that the question has gone from something that I loved answering to a question that almost immediately puts me on edge, because I know what the person is really wanting to know, and once I answer, I feel as if they think they know who I am, based solely on my face. I am proud of my mixed identity, but when people constantly ask me where I am from, I feel like an exhibit, a peculiarity, just something that has to be figured out."

"Alexa" is also mixed—partly White and partly Japanese. In addition to comments based on her partly Japanese look, it is common for her to be identified as not White enough nor Asian enough to fit either category. This implies, she writes, that she is below the standard of both categories.

"Alexa's" description of her reaction to the microaggressions she receives is that "more often than not I feel sad and disappointed because I realize that they stem from people not understanding me as a whole person and jumping to conclusions based on social stereotypes. When friends comment on my appearance, they are unintentionally dubbing me as an outsider who is below the standard of normalcy. This creates doubt about my inherent worth as a human being, a doubt that is made worse by the presence of Christianity within the relationship. When people in positions of authority use their authority to justify microaggressions, I get angry, especially when they are in the church. Their microaggressions raise the question of how to maintain peace with those who do not realize the deep-seated harm they are causing. I usually choose to keep anger to myself, because I see that it would be a losing battle to say something, a battle that would create division where unity is needed. But keeping anger to myself takes a toll on my sense of worth, because it makes me wonder whether what I do could be done better by a person who is unhindered by race."

On Being a Student of Color

"Annie" reflects on her experience as a minority student: "We minority students all have different experiences on campus, and, sadly, a lot of them are hurtful, due to the fact that too often we are recipients of insults, shockingly ignorant remarks, microaggressions, and statements that devalue or completely invalidate our home culture or ethnic makeup. I think that we humans like to put people into familiar boxes or categories, and many students on campus, most of them White, don't have very articulate or well-informed boxes to place minority students in.

"There is not a lot of explicit racism on campus, but implicit racism bleeds out through subtle microaggressions, often masked in the confusing cover of humor. Microaggressions are a type of bullying. They may be camouflaged or partly unintentional, but the feelings of being labeled as weird or 'less than' sting. It is difficult to be studying, working, and living on a campus where you don't feel welcome due to something about your background that you cannot control."

Trevor states, "Being a male of color on campus is no easy task." As a result of the microaggressions he has received, Kyler says, "The most prevalent emotion that I have felt throughout my time at college is being misunderstood." "Ethan's" take on microaggressions is that "they obviously make people uncomfortable and therefore cause people to stay clear of racial discussion." When "Asha" tried to remember some of the many microaggressions she had experienced, she found that she could not state them verbatim. It was as if, she says, her "brain purged them after I vented or fumed in the moment, in order for me to cope and not grow bitter."

Caroline wonders, "Do I have a right to be upset by these seemingly small things or am I making a big deal out of nothing? Do I need to put aside my own feelings and be accommodating so that other people feel comfortable?" She also asks, in a different vein, "Do I owe a response when asked questions that White people would not normally be asked?"

On Being White

In listening to the feelings of minorities about the microaggressions they have experienced, I could not help but ask myself, "How would I feel if I were a person of color who was the recipient of them?" After a period of time, I think I would find it exhausting to have to invest emotional energy in dealing with the microaggressions. With Annie, I might feel very unknown and, again with her, ask, "Why am I at a school where there are all these White people who don't understand and say dumb things?" Perhaps I would wonder whether other students know what they are doing. But as soon as I wondered this I would think of the distinction between genuine and culpable ignorance. With the former, one cannot help being ignorant, but with the latter, one is responsible for being ignorant. I might think, "Why don't they know better? Why haven't they thought of the Golden Rule and asked themselves how they would feel if they were Black, Hispanic, Asian, or some other person of color?"

I have sometimes been the recipient of unkind remarks, but never have I been the recipient of a remark based on my being White, nor am I ever likely to be as long as I inhabit a predominantly White culture. A fair share of my Whiteness consists of the fact that I have not experienced the microaggressions that people of color have experienced. In particular:

The Uneasy Conscience of a White Christian

1. No one has ever touched my hair, or asked to touch it, because they want to know what it feels like.
2. No one has ever assumed that I like a certain kind of music. People always ask, "What kind of music do you like?"
3. No one has ever commented on the way I talk.
4. I have never heard car doors being locked when I walk by someone of a different race sitting in their car.
5. I have never seen people cross the street when they see me.
6. No one has ever directed a racial slur toward me.
7. No one has asked me whether I am a college professor because I am White.
8. No one has ever presumed that I speak for all White people.
9. No one has ever asked me whether English is my first language.
10. No one has made assumptions about the food I eat because I am White.
11. No one has made a comment about how I look because of my skin color or facial configuration.
12. No one has expressed untoward curiosity about the culture of which I am a part.
13. No one has stared at me as I walk around campus as though I don't belong.

In general,

1. I have never been made to feel "less than" because of my race.
2. I have not been fearful of being the recipient of racially motivated remarks.
3. I have not had to invest emotional energy in dealing with comments based on the fact that I am White.
4. Part of my having White privilege involves my not being the recipient of microaggressions.
5. I am usually not aware that I am not the recipient of microaggressions.

This last point needs some unpacking. Part of what is involved in my being White is that I have not been aware that I am White. My being White has felt normal to me. This is because I am part of the dominant racial group in the United States. Moreover, in the White schools and churches I have attended, and in my family of origin, I have not been taught to recognize my feeling of normalcy, nor to be aware of the fact that no one has ever slurred me for being White. I might have become aware of this last fact if I had been taught that people of color are sometimes slurred. But I had not been taught this. As a result, I came to regard my being White, and with it the fact of not having been the recipient of microaggressions, as an "unearned asset which I can count on cashing each day, but about which I was 'meant' to remain oblivious," to use the words of Peggy McIntosh in her classic article, "White Privilege: Unpacking the Invisible Knapsack."[126]

I am no longer oblivious about microaggressions. The invisible has become visible to me. Yet I tend to go through my days largely forgetting that people of color go through their days having to field comments that make them feel unwelcome and disvalued.

I forget too that because it is—to use Trevor's words—"no easy task to be a person of color" on campus, people of color face challenges stemming from realities that I take for granted: a skin color that is not perceived as other, a stable sense of self-worth, welcoming acceptance by those of different races, an unchallenged cultural identity, conversations that are free of unwarranted assumptions about me. I can be confident and comfortable, whereas people of color experience uncertainty and distress.

What to Do?

Perhaps some White people will respond to these lists of microaggressions by wanting to clam up when talking to a person of color for fear of offending them by a stray remark. However, one need not have such fear. There are things one can keep in mind when talking to a person of color. Here are a few:

1. Think of the Golden Rule: imagine that you are a different color or race and ask how you would feel if you were the recipient of a particular question or statement.
2. Exhibit welcoming acceptance.
3. Curb your curiosity. Do not try to find out what "box" to put someone in.

4. Do not assume that you are normal and that the other is not.
5. For those who identify as Christian: picture yourself acting with the same care and respect that Jesus would display.

Actually, these are things to keep in mind when talking to anyone. The point is to treat others, whether like us or not, with the same sensitivity and respect with which we would want to be treated.

It may be too that some people will regard the whole subject of racial microaggressions, and with it the talk of race itself, as unnecessary, perhaps even harmful, to racial harmony. If we simply treat everyone equally, they might say, the issue of race in the United States will be resolved. However, this overlooks the fact that people of color continue to be deeply hurt by microaggressions—even more so, Donald Wing Sue has found, than when they are the object of overt and hateful attacks.[127] In order for people of color to be treated equally, microaggressions must be eliminated from interactions with them. Since people often are unaware of their microaggressions, they must learn about them. One good way to do this is to listen empathetically to those who have been recipients of microaggressions, either in one-on-one encounters or by reading their stories.

Ana

Being Latina in the United States

Ana was born in Venezuela and moved to the United States with her family when she was four. She lives in Illinois and was twenty-seven when we talked.

When I was in fourth grade, I wondered whether people could tell that I was not American. I asked other students, "When you look at me, can you tell that I'm Latina?" A lot of students said, "Yes, of course." I said, "How? I don't know what you're seeing. I look like you, don't I?" They said, "No, you look different."

Some years earlier, I had come home from school with a picture I had drawn of myself with blue eyes. I asked my mom when I would grow blue eyes, as though that was a normal thing. She said, "You're never going to have blue eyes. That's never going to happen." I asked, "Why? Why don't I get those?"

I was shocked by my mom's answer, because I didn't feel that I was different from the other kids at school. I didn't feel Latina. So it was confusing that someone could tell from the way I looked that I am Latina. My mom says I cried when she told me, but I don't remember that.

Later, I became proud of my brown hair and brown eyes. At times I even highlighted features that make me look Latina—my brown hair can be very big and curly. But in elementary school, when I realized that people could tell I am Latina just by looking at me, I felt as though power had been taken from me. For people already to know something about me just by seeing my face made me feel that they had an upper hand. They could see something in me that I wasn't able to see in them.

Also, when I was in elementary school, my dad bought tickets for him and my mom for a concert. But my mom got sick at the last minute and couldn't go. So my dad decided to take me instead. The concert was by Celia Cruz, a well-known Cuban musician and singer. I fell completely in love with her music, which I had not heard anywhere else except at home. I practiced singing her songs, because I thought that one day we would play them at school. I told other students that we went to the concert, but no one knew what salsa music is and no one knew of the musician. I realized then that the music was not going to be played at school. And I also realized that my ethnicity is different from my race. I had thought of myself as White then, but discovered that my culture is different.

In high school, I was one of five Latino students in a school of two thousand. At times, other students bullied me. I got lots of mean comments about having a large butt and about how my hair is curly. It is considered very Latina to have a big behind and curly hair, so those comments were racialized. Also, I was never considered very pretty in high school. That too felt racialized, because I was just different from everyone else. I was pretty, but in a different way.

My parents have not felt fully welcome in the United States, and because of that I don't feel fully welcome either. My parents used to own a home in the suburbs of a large city, and often people wouldn't believe that they did, or they would ask what their apartment number was when they gave out their address. Sometimes my mom can't fully explain what she wants to say in English, so people can't understand her and they assume she's dumb. Once she and I went to Walmart and she paid in cash with a twenty-dollar bill. The cashier gave her change as though she had paid with a ten. My mom immediately said, "Hey! You shorted me. Can you please give me the rest of the money?" The cashier flat out told her, "I didn't think you would be able to count." I was livid. I thought, "Wow! What do my parents experience when I'm not around?"

When I was in college, my dad was laid off from his job, and my parents sold their house and moved into an apartment. After I graduated from college and had worked for a while, we decided to share an apartment. I discovered that it was a whole different experience trying to rent as a Latino family versus renting as an individual. People sometimes said, "Oh, you can skip the Social Security portion of the application if that's a problem for you." Or they hinted that we didn't make enough money, when we had way more than enough, or that we were not in the United States through legal means, or that we would bring problems.

I currently work at a tech company. One of the reasons I wanted to work at it is that it has a great deal of diversity. There is an open office plan, so everybody is together. A lot of people talk in different languages. I find that very welcoming. Earlier, I had an internship at a company where it was very clear that I shouldn't speak Spanish on the phone. People looked at me when I did or walked near my desk and coughed. The majority of the people at the company I work at now speak more than one language, and that makes a big difference to me.

People are sometimes surprised at what I do for a living or at how nice my apartment or neighborhood is. Sometimes I wonder where that surprise comes from. I graduated from college with pretty good grades. I've followed all the right steps that other people have followed. So I don't understand the surprise. Sometimes I think it's because people think that Latina women can't do certain things.

I consider the United States my home, but I don't feel that I belong here. There are people who welcome me here, but I don't feel welcomed. I feel very in between because I'm so connected to my parents, who are very connected to Venezuela, and I have family there. So I feel a constant push and pull. I don't feel that I belong there or here.

10

Is Racial Equity a Conservative or a Liberal Concern?

A FORMER STUDENT WROTE recently, "Most colleges have started lurching to the left politically, which is a real shame since the point of college is to learn to think for oneself and be exposed to different types of speech and expression. So I'm not sure I would agree with the content of your Race and Justice course."

I had not thought of the Race and Justice course I taught as either conservative or liberal, so I was puzzled to see it thought of as liberal. Equity, I had thought, is blind to politics. Upon reflection, two things occurred to me: some of the ideas connected with racial equity in the United States have a conservative-liberal divide, yet conservatives and liberals can, and should, agree on a number of important points. First, some differences.

One difference is over who is responsible for rectifying racial inequity. Conservatives generally say that individuals should rectify it—people of color, especially those who are Black, need to seize opportunities more, and White people need to have the right attitudes toward people of color. If White people are racists, they need to have a change of heart, which is the foundation for changed behavior.

Liberals, however, generally want federal and state governments to rectify racial inequity. Waiting for everyone to change their heart is too slow, they say. It may, in fact, never happen, and even if it did, a change of heart does not always lead to proper behavior. Even more important,

Is Racial Equity a Conservative or a Liberal Concern?

liberals say, racial inequity is manifested in public, institutional, and corporate ways in addition to individual ways. The policies and practices of groups, governmental and nongovernmental, need to change, and this can happen only when they are coerced to do so by law or explicit policy.

This difference is connected to another difference. Conservatives generally believe that the primary cause of racism, and social ills generally, is due to individual actions. Individuals make up social groups and corporate entities, such as businesses, governments, and churches. So it is individuals who are responsible for what social groups do. They need to change in order for the social groups to change.

Liberals, on the other hand, generally believe that racism is due primarily to social causes, that is, to corporate and systemic practices. These are commonly said by liberals to be the main cause of racial inequity in the United States. The racially discriminatory practices and policies of corporate entities go beyond what individuals in the entities do. Institutional racism is the chief culprit of racial inequity.

Conservatives also do not think that people of color should think of themselves as victims, because that would undermine their sense of responsibility to make their lives better. When you think of yourself as a victim, you tend to blame victimizers for your condition and thus believe that they are the ones who need to change, not you. And this is an abdication of the responsibility to change your own life.

Liberals, however, constantly refer to people of color as victims. They have been enslaved, lynched, prevented from voting, excluded in various ways, and discriminated against in jobs, education, housing, and incarceration. Liberals believe that people of color cannot exercise responsibility in these domains until they are no longer recipients of racial harm.

These differences erupted into a shouting match one day in one of my Race and Justice classes. "Michael," a White male, declared that he doesn't think the federal government should do anything to ensure equal education for people of color, or anything to guarantee equal opportunities for jobs or housing. "Faith," a Black female, immediately responded with a raised voice, "What? You don't think anything should be done about racism?" Michael replied, "I don't think the federal government should do those things." Faith shouted, "Are you a racist? Don't you believe that things need to change?!" Michael's plaintive reply was, "Look, I am against racism as much as you are. I just don't think the government should be involved in trying to fix it." He did not come to the next class period.

The Uneasy Conscience of a White Christian

The beliefs of conservatives and liberals could be reconciled if conservatives were willing to admit that systemic racial inequity has handicapped people of color to a great extent and if liberals were willing to admit that personal responsibility plays a role even for victimized people. My aim here, however, is not to try to reconcile the two, but to make a second point that has not been mentioned in talk of racial equity: conservatives and liberals can agree on a number of important truths. The two sides, in fact, should agree on these truths.

One of these is that it is important to listen to people of color tell about their experiences of coping with racism.

When I read the book of slave narratives that my wife bought for me at a garage sale four decades ago, I was deeply moved. There were graphic descriptions of beatings and rapes. Restrictions of basic liberties were detailed—families torn apart, education denied, travel restricted. "Oh!" I thought. "This is what slaves went through."

I, of course, knew about slavery. But it was merely abstract and impersonal knowledge, not concrete and up close. The same was true of my knowledge of other racial inequities. I had heard of segregation and lynchings, but had not been acquainted with individual effects of segregation or seen pictures of lynchings. If I had any knowledge of Emmett Till's murder, it had been very minimal. This was also true of my knowledge of the conditions of Native Americans, Hispanics, and Asian Americans.

There is an important difference between knowing about racial inequities and listening to those who are damaged by it. When knowing about racial inequities, one encounters statistics, patterns, and social conditions. When listening to those who are damaged by racial inequity, one encounters pain, loss, and injury. Knowing statistics, patterns, and social conditions is needed, but it can keep one at a distance from individual responses to racial inequity. Listening to individual responses decreases that distance considerably. It did that again as I listened to the stories of Joi, Beth, Jonathan, Devlin, Israel, Ana, and Lisa.

When you listen to someone who is in pain, you can scarcely avoid feeling their pain. When you listen to someone who has been unjustly discriminated against, you cannot easily prevent yourself from feeling their anger at having been violated. When you listen to someone who has been denigrated or mistreated because of their race, you are likely to feel strongly the need for fair and equitable treatment.

Is Racial Equity a Conservative or a Liberal Concern?

Listening is important because it helps remove the "vast veil" that shuts out people of color from the White world.[128] It brings White people into contact with the realities that are behind the statistics, patterns, and social conditions of racial inequity. This contact reveals what people of color experience when they are unjustly harmed. Both conservatives and liberals should be able to agree on the importance of this contact, simply because it is the sharing of one human's suffering with another.

Conservatives and liberals should also be able to agree that the suffering of American people of color has been grievous. It has been both extensive and intensive. It has been extensive because it has reached into nearly every aspect of their lives—employment, education, housing, incarceration, and everyday interactions with White Americans. It has been intensive because it has often produced acute pain and death.

Both conservatives and liberals should be able to agree that suffering still occurs, in varying degrees. The statistics and anecdotes regarding differential treatment and conditions that are listed in chapter 7 are easily found—in health care, life expectancy, wealth, education, income, arrests, death penalty, and more. There is, to be sure, a difference between conservatives and liberals over the presumed cause of the differential treatment and conditions: conservatives tend to emphasize poverty, class, and lack of individual initiative more than racism, while liberals tend to emphasize systemic racism more than poverty and class or lack of individual initiative. However, both conservatives and liberals should be able to agree that, though a number of factors play a role in differential treatment and conditions, racism nearly always plays some role, which sometimes is fairly large. Current statistics regarding differential treatment and conditions are too extensive, accounts of individual racial discrimination are too numerous, and the history of racial inequity is too long to say that racism has only a little or no role in current racial inequities.

Conservatives and liberals should be able to agree that one aspect of the harm done to people of color is emotional. Cornel West writes that "neither liberals nor conservatives dare to tread into the murky waters of despair and dread that now flood the streets of black America."[129] Christopher Lebron argues that those who are recipients of racial inequity often wrestle with a sense of being less valuable.[130] In his *Less than Human*, David Livingstone Smith documents how African Americans have been dehumanized.[131]

Conservatives and liberals should be able to agree that racism is both explicit and implicit. Explicit racism occurs when deliberate and overt racial inequity is expressed, such as in White nationalism, redlining, the use of racial slurs, or in Ku Klux Klan rallies. Implicit racism occurs when racial harm is produced without explicit intention, such as in facial expressions, words, or policies that unintentionally discriminate. The explicit racism in law, public policy, and nongovernmental organizations, both can agree, has diminished to some degree since the Civil Rights Era. But implicit racism, both can also agree, still remains to a high degree. Moreover, both can agree that laws prohibiting racial discrimination may not be well enforced and that they do not cover every aspect of racial interaction, including implicit racism. One instance of the latter is the racial microaggressions that people of color are recipients of. The intentions of those expressing microaggressions are far from the hateful attacks of overt racists, and yet the effects can hurt their recipients significantly.

Liberals who concur with these points might argue that they entail the need for extensive political and social engagement. Their argument might go like this:

1. American people of color continue to be recipients of racial harm.
2. Social and political intervention is needed to rectify this harm.
3. Therefore, social and political intervention in racial harm is justified.

Or they might use this argument:

1. Ensuring racial equity should be significant priority in the United States.
2. Social and political programs are needed to ensure racial equity.
3. Therefore, social and political programs for racial equity are justified.

Both conservatives and liberals can agree on the truth of statement 1 in each of these arguments. Statement 2 is where the difference between the two political standpoints lies. The differences I described above are involved in the different stances toward statement 2.

Sometimes, though, conservatives seem to shy away from admitting that people of color continue to be recipients of racial harm or from admitting that racial equity is a significant priority, as though doing so would commit them to the liberal viewpoint contained in statement 2 of each argument. And liberals often seem to pounce on the truths asserted in statement 1 of each argument as though those statements automatically prove their side of the divide, the side that is expressed by statement 2 in each

Is Racial Equity a Conservative or a Liberal Concern?

argument. Liberals also may infer that conservatives do not concur with the first statement in each argument because they do not assent to statement 2.

Both conservatives and liberals are mistaken. The second statement in each argument is not entailed by statement 1. The two second statements need to be argued for on grounds different from those that support each statement 1. The arena of the debate between conservatives and liberals should be statement 2 and not statement 1.

Liberals may say that statement 1 in each argument entails statement 2 because the kind of harm involved in racial inequity is systemic. It involves patterns of behavior, not just the attitudes, emotions, and actions of individuals. So the remedy for racial harm must itself involve patterns, which means that the remedy requires the adoption of policies and laws that ensure equitable treatment.

Conservatives' response to this liberal argument will be that even though racial harm involves system-wide patterns of behavior, the way to change those patterns is to change the attitudes, emotions, and actions of individuals in the systems and institutions that manifest racist patterns. If everyone in an institution, governmental or nongovernmental, changed their attitudes and refrained from racially injurious actions, there would be no racist patterns or system-wide racism, they would say.

The reason for this difference between conservatives and liberals lies mainly in the individualist conceptual framework that conservatives generally adhere to and the systemic conceptual framework that liberals generally adhere to. It is individuals, conservatives say, who act. It doesn't make sense to say that institutions act apart from individuals in the institutions. So it is individuals who must take on the responsibility to act in nonracist ways. On the contrary, liberals say, it does make sense to say that institutions act above and beyond the actions of individuals in the institutions. An individual's acting in accordance with an institution's pattern just is an action of the institution. So it is not just individuals who are responsible for racist actions, but institutions as well. This altercation between conservatives and liberals means that it is statement 2 in each of the above arguments that is the bone of contention.

Much could be said about these two frameworks. My point here, though, is that advocates of these different frameworks can agree that American people of color continue to suffer harm as a result of their color and that racial equity should be a significant priority in the United States. Both conservatives and liberals, in fact, should acknowledge these, because they are true, and also because doing so would go some way toward healing the racial alienation that continues to be a prominent part of American life. Conservatives will add to this acknowledgement that the remedies should be individual, whereas liberals will add that the remedies should be largely social and political.

It needs to be noted, though, that it is sometimes not clear whether the silence of conservatives about racial equity is due to their disagreeing with statement 1 in each argument or with statement 2. It may be that their silence is an indication that they believe racial equity is not very important compared to limited government, individual liberties, lower taxes, reducing or eliminating abortion, and having a strong military. Many liberals probably regard this silence as indicating that conservatives hold that belief. And in many cases they would be right. However, the silence of conservatives about racial equity could be due to their regarding racial equity to be largely an individual matter, just as compassion, kindness, and graciousness are individual matters, which generally are not legislated. Politicians and others concerned with social and political matters do not say much about these latter virtues, and by parity of reasoning, conservatives can say, politicians are not obliged to say much about the former. Given this uncertainty, the point I want to make is that conservatives and liberals *can* and *should* agree on a number of things connected with statement 1 in each argument, though they may not actually do so.

My own sentiments are a balance between liberal and conservative, with a shift sometimes one way and sometimes the other way, depending on the issue. Racial equity is an important issue; it is a public, social, and political matter in addition to an individual matter; and it needs social and political remedies in addition to individual remedies. Though conservatives are right to say that attitudes, emotions, and behavior of individuals are important, liberals are right to say that laws and policies of governmental and nongovernmental institutions need to be adopted and enforced to secure racial equity. The history of the United States shows pretty conclusively that if racial matters had been left only to individuals, or to individual states, the United States would still be mired in racism that is worse than currently exists. To be sure, conservatives are right to say that individuals need to adopt nonracist convictions and behavior to bring about widespread change. And recipients of racial harm, each of them, individually, must exercise responsibility to make of their lives what they can. But that responsibility often bumps up against still-existing racial inequities, and it is limited by laws and policies that seem neutral with respect to race but that have harmful racial effects. So it is necessary, though not sufficient (as liberals seem sometimes to suppose), that governments—local, state, and federal—enact laws and policies that ensure racial equity. On the individualist approach, all, or nearly all, individuals in a nation would have to adopt nonracist convictions and behavior in order for racial equity to exist in that nation. This, sadly, is an unrealistic expectation.

As one who balances liberal and conservative approaches, I often find myself thinking that conservatives do not generally rank racial equity high on their list of priorities. Even if I am right in thinking this, I have to remind myself that some of them may have it as a high individual priority without having it as a high social or political priority. The differences between liberals and conservatives, though, should not blur the fact that both should agree on some significant truths with regard to race—that listening to people of color is important, that the harm experienced by people of color has been grievous, that this harm still occurs, that part of the harm people of color experience is emotional, and that racism is both explicit and implicit.

Lisa

Belonging

Lisa was in her early fifties when I talked with her. She lives in Georgia.

WHEN I WAS EIGHT, I went to a Christian camp in Lake Geneva, Wisconsin, for a week, and I was the only Black person at the camp. I loved being there, but it was a very lonely week. I couldn't go the following summer with my Black friends, whom I had invited at the beginning of the summer, because I came down with chicken pox the day before I was supposed to go. But I went by myself a few weeks later. Again, I was the only Black person. The adults and counselors gave me good attention, but among the campers I felt left out, all by myself.

In high school, I spent my whole summers at camp. There were other Blacks at them, and I had a good experience so far as Blacks and Whites were concerned. I bonded well with the other teenagers.

I went to a predominantly White Christian college. During my freshman, sophomore, and junior years, a bunch of Black girls and I got really tight. But they transferred to different colleges after my junior year so that in my fourth year I was the only Black person left from my group of friends. It was a very lonely time.

I was part of the college's concert choir, and after my friends left I was the only Black person in the choir. During spring breaks, we toured different parts of the country. While we were on tour after my friends left, I saw that I was not connecting with the others, and no one was taking the initiative to connect with me. Before we sang at churches on the tours we went on, we had a time of talking and testimony and prayer. One of these times I said, "It's been uncomfortable for me this year because I have felt left out. And no one has noticed that."

It was a hard thing for me to confront the whole group in this way. But I felt good after I said it, because I made them aware that they had their own world and they were not including me in that world. No one was welcoming me and making me feel that I belonged.

For most of my life the churches I have gone to have been all Black. When I was seven, my daddy became pastor of a church on the south side of Chicago, and I went there until I got married at twenty-six. In Georgia, where my husband is from, we were part of several Black churches over a period of seventeen years. In 2013, the congregation we were then in merged with a much larger, predominantly White church.

When we first moved to this church, I wasn't connecting with the people in it, as though I was just another person for them to skip over. The people didn't feel welcoming or accepting, and I felt out of place. Then I realized that I needed not to make everything about myself and that I needed to initiate connecting with them, almost like forcing myself into their world to get to know them.

Now my husband and I are members of a small group that meets once a month on second Fridays. There are six in the group, half Black and half White. We started the group in September of 2020, after George Floyd was killed in Minneapolis, so that we could talk about the problem of racism in the US. We are going through issues based on a discussion guide from an organization called Be the Bridge.

People in the group are being honest. The discussions have, I think, opened the eyes of the Whites in the group to see that there are things that they aren't aware of or that they need to work on.

A lot of times we Blacks feel that the United States belongs to White America. When we Blacks are in spaces with White people, we, both Blacks and Whites, are not in that space all together. Rather, we Blacks are in their space. Also, sometimes I feel that when we Blacks say something, Whites feel that they have to come along after us and give the final word, the final answer, about what their thoughts are on the subject. Everything hinges on what they decide—they don't take the time to find out what we Blacks have to offer. That's when I feel the White supremacist attitude comes in. When it does, it doesn't feel that we are coming together in equal parts. It feels like a hierarchy, with Blacks on the bottom of it.

I want for us to get to a spot where we are able to brainstorm and figure things out together. The small group my husband and I are part of is helping us to see that we all have something to add and something to give so that we all have equal status. We are getting to the place where everybody can be heard equally.

Recently, there have been two panel discussions about race for the whole church. The Blacks on the panel were asked to share about events in their lives when they had been the recipients of racism, and the Whites in the church got to see what it feels like to be a Black person in the United States. Since then I have noticed that some of the White people in the church have been making an effort to check in and say hello when they see me. And some have invited me to lunch. They share what they are thinking about racism in the US or in our church or in their world. And I share my view.

Something else that has helped keep us all together as an integrated church is that during the Sunday service it is said from the front of the church that we accept each other as Christ has accepted us. Before the COVID pandemic of 2020 and 2021, we had a time during the service when we greeted each other with hugs and warm greetings.

Also, there are small groups, different from the Be the Bridge group we are in, where we bond with each other and get to know one another and come around the gospel and disciple one another. These small groups are where we build unity and do life together.

Each group has a missional focus. We reach out to the community to try to win others for Christ or do some kind of ministry for the neighborhood. The group my husband and I are in reaches out to a nearby orphanage and provides things they need for the kids in it. I feel that I'm connecting to the Blacks and Whites in our group, and that is bringing us together. The church is growing.

11

The Resistance of Southern Whites to the 1961 Freedom Rides

THE DETAILS OF THE 1961 Freedom Rides are exhaustively described in Raymond Arsenault's *Freedom Riders: 1961 and the Struggle for Racial Justice* and vividly depicted in a two-hour documentary film, *Freedom Riders: American Experience.*[132] Long after one finishes reading the book and watching the film, one still recalls the melee in which Southern Whites wielded baseball bats and steel pipes to attack the riders as they disembarked from their bus at a Birmingham bus station. One cannot forget the smoke and flames that spread throughout the very first freedom bus as a result of a fire bomb that was tossed into it through an already broken window.

There were 436 riders. Some were college students, some were ordinary citizens, and a few were ministers. Nearly half were from the South, and a little more than half were from the North.

The rides usually began in a Northern city and ended in Montgomery, Birmingham, Jackson, or New Orleans. They were done on Greyhound and Trailways buses, plus a few on train. The impetus for the rides was a recent Supreme Court decision that made segregation in interstate travel illegal (*Boynton v. Virginia*, 1960). The riders made sure that they bought tickets to a city in a different state from which they departed.

Intrastate segregation, however, was not affected by the Supreme Court's decision. But the distinction between intrastate and interstate travel was of no significance to Southern states. They did not want the federal

The Uneasy Conscience of a White Christian

government intruding in their traditional way of life, which, they believed, ensured harmony between White folks and Black folks. The "they" included local and state judges, police, government officials, bus drivers, church people, ordinary citizens, and members of the White Citizens Council.

Segregation on buses meant that White people sat in front and Black people in back. It also meant that bus stations had separate waiting rooms, restaurants, and water fountains. Prominently displayed signs, in all caps, indicated which was which:

- VIRGINIA STATE LAW REQUIRES ALL COLORED PASSENGERS TO RIDE IN REAR OF BUS
- NO DOGS NEGROES MEXICANS
- WAITING ROOM FOR COLORED ONLY, BY ORDER POLICE DEPT.
- DRINKING FOUNTAIN (two of them near each other), with WHITE and an arrow underneath it pointing to the left, and COLORED and an arrow underneath it pointing to the right

The Freedom Riders usually traveled in groups of six to ten. The White riders in each group sat in the back of the bus, the Black riders in the front, and one rider was a designated observer, who sat in the "proper" space of the bus. When arriving at a station, the White riders went to a colored-designated bathroom or restaurant, and the Black riders went to a White-designated bathroom or restaurant.

It is more accurate to say that the Black Freedom Riders tried to sit in the front of the buses and tried to use White-designated bathrooms or station restaurants. Sometimes they succeeded, but sometimes they did not. When Black Freedom Riders sat down in the front of a bus, they were often asked by the bus driver to go to the back. When the riders refused, sometimes the police were called and the riders removed from the bus and arrested.

The author of *Freedom Riders* writes, "Emboldened by defiant White Citizens' Council leaders and demagogic politicians, individual bus drivers, station agents, and police officers routinely ignored federal mandates, dismissing them as illegitimate infringements of local control and states' rights."[133]

Both the book and the film display, in raw particularity, the strenuous resistance of Southern Whites to desegregation.

The Resistance of Southern Whites to the 1961 Freedom Rides

- A Greyhound bus headed to New Orleans from Washington, DC, has some of its windows smashed at the bus station in Anniston, Alabama, by angry White protesters. After the bus leaves the Anniston station, it is stopped six miles later by more angry White residents. Someone throws a flaming bundle of rags through one of the broken windows while the riders are still in it. Fortunately, they all escape before the bus is consumed by fire and smoke, but some are badly injured.[134]

- Birmingham police officers inform local Klansmen that they will not be at the Trailways bus station for the first fifteen minutes after a bus with Freedom Riders in it arrives. During those fifteen minutes, riders are punched, kicked, dragged, and beat. No Klansman is arrested.[135]

- In the Montgomery Greyhound station, Freedom Riders are greeted first by a "group of white men armed with lead pipes and baseball bats" and shortly later by a "surging mob" carrying "baseball bats, wooden boards, bricks, chains, tire irons, pipes, even garden tools—hoes and rakes."[136] John Seigenthaler, deputy assistant to Robert Kennedy, the US attorney general, approaches the scene with horror and attempts to aid a young White woman who is a Freedom Rider and who is being punched repeatedly in the face. He is hit on the back of his head with a pipe, falls to the ground unconscious, is kicked in the ribs and dragged behind his car, and lies there, still unconscious, for twenty-five minutes before being discovered by a reporter.[137]

- Fourteen students at Tennessee State University are expelled for being Freedom Riders.[138]

- Numerous Freedom Riders, all of whom had been trained to be nonviolent, are arrested for "disturbing the peace" or "disorderly conduct." Many of them serve time in jail or prison, including at Parchman, a Mississippi state penitentiary that is known for its repression of Black inmates. In the early part of the twentieth century, Parchman participated in the practice of convict leasing for farm labor, which was little better than slavery and in some ways worse.

All of this reminds me of a 1968 visit to my grandfather, who lived in Birmingham at the time of the Freedom Rides and who was a minister in a Southern Baptist church there. I went with him to a talk he gave to the youth in a Baptist church on a Sunday evening. I remember none of what he said, except for the declaration, seemingly stuck in the middle of other thoughts, "I believe in segregation. But I don't believe in being cruel about it—'Get around back, n_____!'"

To this day, I am haunted by his assertion. How could one who was so gracious and kind, loved by everyone in the churches he pastored, be a segregationist? It did not matter how uncruel he thought he was being. The whole system of segregation was cruel. He was among the people whom Martin Luther King Jr. had in mind as he wrote his "Letter from a Birmingham Jail" in 1963.

I am similarly haunted by the virulent passion that the White segregationists exhibited in their responses to the Freedom Riders. What was it about integration that angered them so?

One answer is stated in *Freedom Riders*, given by the judges, business owners, police officers, and citizens of Southern states in response to the Freedom Riders: "They are disturbing our way of life." When one has grown up in a starkly segregated context, one is firmly imbued with the values of that context. Change is nearly impossible.

Another answer, given by the author of *Freedom Riders* as he reflects on the resistance the riders encountered, is that White Southerners were not able to feel empathy for the condition of the Black residents in their midst. This was so, he states, because they were rigidly entrenched in an entirely different system of customs and values. This answer is reminiscent of Aleksandr Solzhenityn's famous question in his *One Day in the Life of Ivan Denisovich*: "How can someone who is warm understand one who is cold?," written about the guards in Russian concentration camps.

A further answer, unspoken by anyone in *Freedom Riders*, is that in the segregated culture in the South, White people enjoyed a significant degree of control over Black people. The Freedom Rides threatened to destroy that control. And if there is anything that one fiercely hangs onto when confronted with severe opposition, it is control—or what comes to the same thing, power. Frederick Douglass, a Black spokesperson for Black rights before, during, and after the Civil War, understood this well: "Power concedes nothing without a demand. It never did and it never will."[139]

A last answer is that undoing segregation threatened the very identity of the White people who lived in it. To quote James Baldwin yet again, White people in the United States "have had to believe for many years, and for innumerable reasons, that black men are inferior to white men. . . . The danger, in the minds of most white Americans, is the loss of their identity."[140] Integration, Baldwin is saying, causes White people to lose their

The Resistance of Southern Whites to the 1961 Freedom Rides

identity. The identity that would be lost is their sense of superiority over Black people.

For this reason, Baldwin infers, White people *need* Black people. They need Black people to secure their identity as superior to Black people. So, Baldwin continues, "the black man has functioned in the white man's world as a fixed star, as an immovable pillar: and as he moves out of his place, heaven and earth are shaken to their foundations."[141]

In light of just this last answer, one might be surprised if there had been no resistance to the Freedom Riders. The immovable pillars of the White Southern identity had been shaken and were in danger of falling.

In spite of these answers, I am still haunted by my grandfather's segregationism and the extreme resistance of White Southerners to the Freedom Rides. How can so many people, how can even just one person, harbor so much opposition to the idea of equal treatment for all?

I want to suggest that an even more haunting question is: Don't the above four reasons for the violent responses to the Freedom Riders also explain why racial disparities continue now? In particular, don't they explain why systemic racism still exists and why individual implicit racism remains in so many people? Do we White Americans not feel that our way of life, plus our values, dominance, and even our very identity, are threatened by full and extensive equity?

We White Americans do not want to ask these questions. Our first reaction to the violent resistance is to shake our heads sadly at it. "We are not like them," we say to ourselves, little realizing that the Pharisee in Jesus's parable distinguished himself from thieves and rogues in precisely the same way (Luke 18:11). I have caught myself reacting in this way more than once. This makes me uneasy. I am a typical White Christian, so it seems likely that other White Christians have done the same. And even though the four reasons explain why, this fact is still haunting.

12

How Slavery Affects Us Now

A 2019 POLL BY Pew Research Center found that 63 percent of Americans believe that the legacy of slavery affects the position of Black people in American society today, either a great deal or a fair amount. For Whites, the percentage is 58 percent, while for Blacks, the percentage is 84 percent.[142] My concern here is not with the White-Black disparity, but with the 63 percent. Why do they think that the legacy of slavery has lasted a century and a half? The survey does not say, and I will not speculate. But I will describe three reasons that both White and Black people should have for thinking that slavery still affects us now. These are that the knowledge of slavery should be an integral part of the conception we Americans have of our country, that the way in which we think of US history often affects how we current Americans think of ourselves, and that there are a number of ways in which a causal chain of events leads from slavery to the present.

(1) The writing of history is affected by the values one holds. In particular, the writing of the history of the United States is affected by whether one regards racial inequity as a serious moral, social, and political harm. Historians who do not regard the harm as serious are likely to downplay the role of slavery when writing a history of the United States. This is why "official" histories of the United States have often focused on the ideals advocated by the White (male) founders of the United States—freedom for all to pursue their own ways of living a good life. This freedom plays a dominant role in the official account of the origin of the United States. Because

of this dominant role, Americans who have taken in the official history of the United States think of themselves as inhabiting what the US National Anthem calls "the land of the free and the home of the brave."

A historian who regards racial inequity as a serious harm will point out that this official history undervalues the fact that a significant percentage of people in the United States were forcedly denied the ability to live according to the founding ideals for more than two and a half centuries prior to the Civil War. This fact will have a prominent place in a different conception of what the United States is all about. This different conception is of a country that adopted high ideals at its founding yet explicitly and deliberately prevented a significant percentage of its population from achieving them—almost 700,000 in 1790 (about 18 percent of the total population) and nearly 4,000,000 in 1860 (about 13 percent of the total population). Whereas in the official picture of the country the founders of the United States were advocates and defenders of the revolutionary idea that life, liberty, and the pursuit of happiness belong to everyone, in this different picture the founders inhabited an entirely separate world from those who were denied living out this revolutionary idea. In the official version of the country's ethos, the original Americans were freedom lovers who were willing to defend that freedom from kings and all who would undermine that freedom. In the alternate version, White Americans were willing to defend only their own freedom. They said one thing but participated in something diametrically opposed to it. This was as true of professed Christians as it was of non-Christians.

This different picture of our country with its separate worlds is reinforced by the horrors of slavery—whipping, raping, long work hours, inadequate diets, lack of education, sometimes separated families, substandard housing, restricted travel, disenfranchisement, and more. Solomon Northup, who was born free but was cunningly kidnapped and sold into slavery, wrote about one of his owners that he "was a roystering, blustering, noisy fellow, whose chief delight was in dancing with his 'n_____s,' or lashing them about the yard with his long whip, just for the pleasure of hearing them screech and scream, as great welts were planted on their backs."[143] Harriet Jacobs, who spent seven years in an impossibly small attic space so that she would not be ravished by her owner, described the time when a group of slaves were being taken by wagon to be sold: "And now came the trying hour for that drove of human beings, driven away like cattle, to be sold they knew not where. Husbands were torn from wives, parents from children, never to look upon each other again this side of the grave. There was wringing of hands and cries of despair."[144] These descriptions dramatically display the radical difference between the White free world and the Black slave world.

The economic aspects of slavery reinforce this radical difference even further. Except for a few slaves who were hired out by their owners or who baked food for sale, slaves were not paid for their labor. Nor could they own land, houses, livestock, or businesses. Cotton is what made the United States wealthy, both South and North, but the slaves who produced it could not partake of that wealth to even the slightest degree. They were, in essence, being used to further the interests not only of their owners, but of White culture in general. "Merely used" is a better phrase to describe how the White world related to them. That White world exploited the Black world for its own benefit only.

This different conception of American history is the truer version, because it accounts for more of the important facts. The facts about slavery are important because racial equity is important. In this different conception, the United States was not nearly as unified as the national story portrays. Not everyone was free. There were two radically different worlds with their radically different experiences. The official conception is much prettier, of course. But it must be rejected in favor of one that is a good deal less pretty, in fact, not pretty at all.

I myself grew up with the official version. Because of the way in which it seeped into my mind when I was younger, I bonded with it, and it has taken a good deal of time to let it go. Part of this letting go has involved disentangling the official version from my Christian faith, which, I thought at the time, entailed that I should revere the founders of the United States because of their commitment to freedom. It was not until I realized that their commitment to freedom extended only to other White Americans that I could give up the official version of my country's history.

(2) Both the official conception of US history and the divided conception affect how current Americans conceive of themselves. Those who think of US history in the official way are likely to have a measure of pride for belonging to a country whose founders espoused the revolutionary ideal of freedom for all. "I belong to this great country," they are likely to think. And to think this is to have a certain conception of oneself, for one's self-identity is often formed, in part, by the country one inhabits. (Not always, to be sure.) On the other hand, those who think of US history in the divided way,

How Slavery Affects Us Now

White or Black, are likely to have a measure of shame and dismay, perhaps even anger, for what their country did to slaves: "My country has deliberately and horribly mistreated, violated, and wounded a large number of Black people." This too is to have a certain conception of oneself—"I belong to a country that has done these dreadful things."

Current Black Americans who adopt the divided version of US history are liable to have additional reactions to slavery. They might feel, as AJ does about America now (as stated in the introduction), that for two and a half centuries America did not like people who look like them. They would not regard the White founders of the United States as their unqualified heroes, as those who adopt the official version are likely to do (and as I did). "Your heroes are not my heroes," they might say to people who adopt the official version. Black Americans whose ancestors were slaves could feel somewhat rootless, because they cannot trace their lineage beyond slavery. And they would likely feel a good deal of empathetic pain at the fact that relatives of theirs were so badly treated, in the same way that most of us would feel pained if a great-grandparent had been unjustly jailed.

In general, Black Americans are more likely to have a negative self-conception because of their knowledge of slavery than are White Americans who adopt the official version of US history. It is true, of course, that Black Americans may resist this negative self-conception. If they do, their self-conception will include the idea that they are someone who must resist a negative self-conception, unlike Americans who adopt the official version and who embrace what they regard as the ennobling self-conception that results from adopting that version.

(3) It is sometimes said that slavery has influenced current conditions in the United States merely because there are similarities between the two. That, however, is not enough to establish that slavery has influenced current conditions. A causal chain between then and now must be established. Historians are the best people to speak to this matter, but there is enough accessible information for nonhistorians to say that there are a number of such causal chains. They exist with respect to the major social ways in which Black Americans have been harmed: poverty, housing, jobs, education, and health care. These causal chains are part of a larger picture that goes like this:

Prior to the Civil War, slaves who escaped from the South found that they were not treated in the North as well as they had hoped they would be. Racial discrimination existed there as well as in the South, though of course not to the same degree. After slavery ended in 1865, Reconstruction lasted only twelve years. In the Compromise of 1877, Rutherford Hayes traded votes from Southern senators to secure the presidency in exchange for removal of federal troops from Southern states. When Hayes became president, Southern states undid Reconstruction policies that had benefited former slaves, because federal troops were not there to enforce those policies. Conditions became worse for Black people living in the South, in some ways as bad as slavery, and racial discrimination continued to exist in the North and elsewhere. Southern senators and congressional representatives exerted a great deal of power over national policies so as to preserve the Southern states' right to maintain their own way of life.

Discrimination in the first half of the twentieth century, in both the South and the North, plus the rest of the country, was sustained partly by federal, state, and local laws and policies, as documented by Richard Rothstein in *The Color of Law*, and partly by racial socialization. The Civil Rights Era undid some of that discrimination, but it would be naïve to suppose that the racial discrimination that had been embedded in US social and economic structures, plus its national psyche, came to a sudden halt then. (I myself had thought this for a long time.) Numerous statistics, some of them presented in chapter 7, show that it has remained, some of it overt and some of it covert. Moreover, Christians have contributed to racial discrimination, from slavery times until now, as documented by Jemar Tisby in *The Color of Compromise* and by Willie James Jennings in *The Christian Imagination*.

This third way in which slavery affects us now extends each of the first two ways to the present. Not only do I belong to a country that seriously harmed Black people via slavery, but I belong to a country that still harms them. And this country remains divided in racial ways. My self-conception is formed in part not only by what my country did, but by what it continues to do. Black Americans who think of the United States as divided must wrestle with their self-conception in ways that White Americans who think of the United States in the official, freedom-loving way do not.

An important takeaway from these three ways in which the legacy of slavery affects Black people today is that to understand the current, divided America well, one needs to understand more than the typical US cursory knowledge of what slavery was like. This is a particularly poignant way in which studying history helps one to understand the present.

Jonathan
Church Encounters

Jonathan has had a number of other racialized encounters besides those with police. Here he describes some of them, including those with White churches. He is a football coach and works at a nonprofit organization in the Minneapolis–St. Paul area.

THE MOST RECENT EXPERIENCE I had with a church occurred eight months ago, in May 2020, right after the killing of George Floyd, a Black man who was choked to death by a White police officer in Minneapolis. A lot of the protests took place in the old neighborhoods where elderly folk live. They were becoming desperate because their pharmacies had been destroyed by the riots and fires. So some of us were trying to get medicine and other supplies to them. Actually, we were coordinating for people to buy things and taking those things to places that distributed them. My job was to recruit people. I recruited about 250 volunteers in 48 hours. We were dispersed all over the place, bringing food and everyday items, anything that people needed.

At the time, we were attending a predominantly White church. I tried calling the campus pastor at the church to help us out, but he never responded—not to any phone calls, not to any texts. Three days passed, and the senior pastor put out a video that said, "What happened to George Floyd was very, very tragic. We as a church do not condone looting and burning." My reaction to that was, "Okay. My phone call to you was about helping people, and you have yet to respond to that." It took a month for the campus pastor to get back to me.

As he and I talked, I realized that my greatest frustration when dealing with White Christians—evangelical Christians—is that everything is a conversation to them. But this justice thing is not a conversation. Actual buildings are on fire. Actual people need actual medicine right now. I thought, "How can this be happening in your city and all you do is talk?" The financial resources the church has are unbelievable, yet it took no action. It would have been a drop in the bucket for them to get their vans and drive people to stores so that they could buy things. The church didn't even need to pay for what the people bought. Instead, they had an intellectual exercise that was designed to comfort their White congregation. They invited a Black pastor to do a series of talks. The whole experience was so disagreeable to me, and it was so disagreeable to my wife, who is White, that she said, "We're not going back."

A month later the pastor texted me, and I was so angry that I have yet to read his text. For me it was, "You showed your hand. When it comes down to it, you talk about missions to the rest of the world so that you can pat yourself on the back. You send twenty thousand dollars to build a well in India, but five blocks from you people of color need help and you are nowhere around. All you did then was spend your time talking about ways you could talk about race with your children."

I am still angry. I had the same experience at the Christian college I went to. Students shut down conversations about actual justice with theological hypotheticals. They'd say, "Oh, that's liberation theology." I'd say, "No, we're just trying to feed people. I'm pretty sure that's foundational to biblical principles. We're just trying to feed people." I had this happen numerous times, at college and at churches, and it always came down to a thought exercise: "We need to have a conversation about race." "No, you need to take action about this."

For me, the lack of my church's response was, "Here we are again. It's just discussion." It was incredibly painful to me that the church opted simply to soothe its wounds when it realized that there was a gap between itself and what needed to be done.

We did not leave that church just because of this one incident, in isolation. We had experienced a number of racialized events over the years, in church and out, that made this incident the final straw.

Jonathan

Shortly after we got married, we were in a grocery store shopping. A man who was probably in his late forties saw us and said, "You're disgusting." He was saying that being a mixed couple is disgusting to him. We passed him again and he said the same thing. After about the fifth time of this, my wife was getting riled up. I said to her, "Listen, if you say something to him, he's going to get aggressive, I'm probably going to have to knock him out, and then I'll have to go to jail. You just have to let this go." This was the first time she had been the target of something like that and it shook her quite a bit. The guy was not quiet. He started out quiet, but every time he saw us he let us know that we are disgusting.

Later, in a small town in Wisconsin, where nearly everyone is White, a sequence of events prompted us not only to leave my job, but to leave the town. I was running a program at the college there. One of the students who did graphic design for my department is Mexican, from Texas. As she was walking to the college one day, a truck full of White guys drove by and threw full cans of beer at her while chanting, "Build that wall! Build that wall!" They were referring to the border wall between the United States and Mexico that Donald Trump had promised to build if he were to become president.

Another time, a Black student of mine was in the shower at the college dorm, and a bunch of White students came into the bathroom barking at him and poured dog food on him while he was showering.

In the summer, during one of the free times in the precollege program I ran, some of the Black girls in the program were just outside the dorm doing double Dutch—jumping rope with two ropes. Someone called the campus police. The police said, "We weren't sure there was an adult here." I said, "There's three supervising adults right here." The police said, "We really couldn't tell." I said, "I'm telling you now that there's three supervising adults here, so you all can go away."

Our oldest son was in first grade at the time, and he lost his winter gloves at the school in town. So my wife went with him to look in the lost and found. The principle followed them back to the parking lot. My wife said, "Can we help you?" The principal said, "I was just making sure he didn't steal anything."

Then came the last incident. Our first-grader had been having issues with the way his teacher interacted with him. One day I went to pick him up. The students have to give a little slip to a teacher when their parent comes so that the school knows that the right kid leaves with the right parent. The parent gives the slip to the child, and the child gives it to a teacher.

The Uneasy Conscience of a White Christian

When I arrived, our first-grader saw me before the teacher who was waiting with him did. He ran to me and reached out for the slip. The teacher, though, slapped his hand away. I was incensed. "Hey! You're messing with my kid. Under federal law I'm not free to tell you what I would do if you were to do that again. But don't do it again." She brushed it off. It didn't bother her that I had seen her do it.

When I told my wife about this, we both said, "We have to get out of here." We had dealt with the dog food episode and all the other events, and now it was smacking things out of the hands of first-graders. When we complained, they didn't respond. We just got tired of contending with these aggressive experiences. Eventually, it was going to get more aggressive. So we got out of there as fast as was humanly possible. That was only four years ago, in 2016.

Back to churches. I have been to a lot of White churches. They have no problem with my playing music or putting me over music. They love for me to play, but they don't want to hear a message about using their privileges that come with being White for the benefit of those who are not. They don't like being made to feel that they aren't doing enough. But that's the truth. When I push them actually to do the gospel, I'm considered liberal or something.

Once I had a conversation with a White man who was an elder. He said to me, "Sometimes I think you're more Black than Christian." I replied, "I find it interesting that you think you're not more White than Christian, that your Christianity is not formed by your Whiteness, that you believe that what you do is real Christianity and that what I do is Black Christianity. Even the notion that what you're doing is real Christianity is incredibly White."

It has gotten to the point where I refuse to play music in a White church. At this juncture in my life, I see my work as outside the building, because I cannot deal with what goes on inside it. I cannot deal with the White paternalist attitudes. I cannot deal with the lack of engagement. I'm not going to go to a White church, because you eventually bump into this stuff. You will be shut down.

13

Why Church Integration May Never Happen

WHEN A FRIEND POSTED the link to an article titled "Overcoming Racism in the Church" on her Facebook page, an acquaintance of hers replied, "When are we going to understand, it's NOT racism, it's CULTURE!!"

Without denying that different cultural traditions contribute to segregation in US churches, I shall describe some racial causes. It may be impossible to determine how much culture and race have contributed to church segregation, but it is certain that racial considerations have played a large role, at least for people of color.

I want to cast the racial causes of church segregation as an answer to the question, what must happen for there to be integration in US churches? The answer, I believe, is that the following eight considerations must be addressed by White churches. If they are not, it is likely that White churches will stay as segregated as they currently are. Although I will cast several of these considerations in terms of Black Americans, they also are pertinent to Native Americans, Hispanics, and those with Asian ancestry.

(1) *Whiteness:* People of color are aware of the sense of racial normality and superiority that is present in most White Americans. Could they sit in the same pew as people who regard them as not normal and as inferior?

Howard Thurman puts the answer to this question in terms of the Roman and the Jew. In order to worship together, he says, "there had to be a moment when the Roman and the Jew emerged as neither Roman nor Jew, but as two human spirits that had found a mutual, though individual,

The Uneasy Conscience of a White Christian

validation."[145] This mutual validation, Thurman goes on to say, would be impossible to experience "as long as either was functioning only within his own social context"—the Roman "with all the arrogance and power of the dominant group" and the Jew always aware of this "difference and the disadvantage of status."[146]

In the highly racialized United States, it seems nearly impossible for people of color and White people to disengage themselves from their racial context. Whiteness is embedded in the psyche of most White people so deeply that they cannot easily extricate themselves from it, including during the time they spend in church. And the psyche of people of color has embedded in it the view that most White people are entrenched in their Whiteness, so that people of color cannot easily regard themselves as free from the superiority-inferiority context. Thurman, who is aware of these facts, concludes that "in a very tragic sense, the ultimate fate of the relationship [between non-Whites and Whites] seems to be in the hands of the wider social context."[147] The wider social context, which in the United States is infused with Whiteness, thus seems to control who goes to which church.

(2) *Racial disparities:* Black Americans are often aware of the numerous racial disparities that exist between Black and White Americans. These disparities are evident to them in the lower quality of public schools they often attend, the disproportionate number of Black males who are arrested, the disproportionate number of times they are stopped by police while driving, the higher employment rate among them, the lower quality of the neighborhoods they often live in, the wage and wealth gaps between them and White Americans, and many more, as listed in chapter 7.

With this awareness, it is hard to imagine that Black people would feel comfortable even visiting an all-White church. There are so many racial disparities, in dozens of different categories, that it is almost certain that some of the White people in any given mostly White church would be on the other side of those disparities, that is, be the ones who are involved in the disparities. Could Black people worship unhindered by thoughts of oppression in such a context? Perhaps so, but not without some uneasiness.

(3) *Individual responsibility versus social reform:* A high percentage of White conservative and evangelical Christians believe that racism should be dealt with by individuals. A high percentage of Black Christians, however, believe that racism should be dealt with by social reform, which includes for them changing public policy and changing the way social and governmental institutions operate. The social reform people are likely to

regard the individual responsibility people as not taking racism seriously. And the individual responsibility people are likely to regard the social reform people as not focusing on the essence of Christianity, or even missing it, which, they say, is a matter of individual hearts.

In their book *Divided by Faith: Evangelical Religion and the Problem of Race in America*, Michael D. Emerson and Christian Smith explicate this divide extensively.[148] The individual responsibility people regard racism as sin and say that sin is a product of individual choices. The remedy for racism is, accordingly, individual choices and a change of the hearts of individuals. Both the origin and the remedy for racism are matters of theology, according to the individual responsibility people, which means that they believe that social reform people have a deficient theology. Social reform people are missing something essential to Christianity, they say.

The social reform people regard racism primarily as structural, that is, as a product of institutional and governmental laws, policies, and practices. One can have a change of heart about racism, but that by itself, they say, will not change the laws, policies, and practices of the racist system in which US Black and White Americans live. The social reform people regard the individual responsibility approach to racism as misguided, uninformed, and ineffective. They very likely would have a good deal of discomfort being in a church that adopts that approach, and, of course, would not like it if they were told that they are not focusing on something that is essential to Christianity.

(4) *The political priority of abortion:* Again, a high percentage of White conservative and evangelical Christians have different political priorities than most Black Christians. By itself, this does not automatically produce segregation, as a number of congregations have members with different political proclivities. However, those who regard being anti-abortion as supremely important have almost always regarded being anti-racist as less important. That is, stamping out abortion has been held by most White conservative and evangelical Christians as more important, probably much more important, than eliminating racism. This would pretty clearly prompt most Black Christians to steer clear of such congregations.

(5) *White power:* For White people in the United States to hold most of the political, economic, and educational power means that they have most of the positions of authority in a wide array of organizations. These include businesses, governments, schools, and churches. In general, people with positions of authority tend to like being with others who have positions of

authority, and people without such positions tend to like being with others like them. These facts might appear to be only a cultural difference. But that is not the case, as White people in the United States have a disproportionate share of positions of authority compared to people of color. The differences in authority are largely due to a racial difference. The disproportionate share of positions of authority is often true too of churches that are intentionally multiracial. Studies have shown that White people often retain the positions of authority in White churches that have become multiracial.[149] It is not surprising, then, that, though such churches have some degree of racial diversity, people of color might not feel fully welcome in them.

(6) *Microaggressions:* A high percentage of adult people of color have been recipients of microaggressions from White people. Microaggressions are not intended to be hurtful, but they are, in fact, hurtful, especially when they pile up over years. Here is an activity for which results matter more than intention. So it is not appropriate to ask people of color not to mind them because of their nonhurtful intentions. The question to ask White Christians is, would you want to be in an environment, even if for only an hour or an hour and a half a week, in which you fear being emotionally injured by thoughtless comments by those who differ from you?

(7) *Different emotional worlds:* In an important respect, Black and White Americans inhabit different emotional worlds. A high percentage of Black folks fear being stopped by the police and being harmed, or even killed, by them. White folks do not. A higher percentage of Black people worry about money than do White people. A certain percentage of Black Americans are angry that their ancestors were enslaved, lynched, and made to sit in the back of city buses, whereas White Americans do not have cause to be angry in these ways. Many Black people are distressed that they do not have the same quality of public schools for their children as do White people and that they do not have the same opportunities to live where they wish.

There are, no doubt, many emotions that both Black and White Christians have in common, partly because both experience an array of normal human emotions, and partly because both are concerned about emotions emphasized in Christianity, such as remorse and joy. Still, the fact that White Christians do not have the same emotional experiences that many Black Christians have may make some Black Christians feel unappreciated or even alienated when in the presence of those White Christians.

(8) *Safe spaces:* A safe space is one in which people feel unafraid to share their thoughts and feelings with others in that space. It is one in

which people of color do not feel reluctant to communicate their racialized experiences with the White folks they encounter in the space. For this to be the case, White folks must not get defensive when they listen to what people of color say about how they have been mistreated. They must not deny or downplay the importance of what people of color say. They must be willing to listen nonjudgmentally and show by their bodily demeanor that they are paying full attention to what they are hearing. To do these, they must "travel" to the worlds of their non-White friends, as María Lugones describes in chapter 1.

People of color, though, have often been in unsafe spaces and have known White folks to whom they could not trust telling about their racialized experiences. They know that the sense of normality and superiority that many White people have prevents them from setting defensiveness aside. Unless there are intentional discussions of the sort that Lisa and Devlin describe in which racial issues are talked about, people of color are unlikely to enter into full fellowship with White churchgoers. Some will feel alienated and stay in their own churches.

One way of getting at the core of what goes on in White churches with respect to these eight considerations is embodied in an assertion that the authors of *Divided by Faith* make: "Even if made up of loving, unselfish individuals, the group transmutes individual unselfishness into group selfishness."[150] Their point is that individuals in White churches can be loving and unselfish toward other White people in those churches, but this becomes group selfishness precisely because the love and unselfishness are directed only to other White people in the churches.

The remedy for group self-centeredness is for people in the group to direct their love and unselfishness to people outside the group. Unfortunately, the eight considerations I have described make it highly unlikely that this will happen to a significant degree in White churches. Any one or two of the eight considerations could well prevent some non-White churchgoers from joining White churches. Is there, then, no hope for integration? Let us look at the options.

One possibility is for White Christians to join non-White churches. This strikes me as likely to have a higher success rate than for people of color joining White churches. However, although the success rate might be higher, it does not seem likely that the amount of White Christians who join non-White churches would be high. There would have to be numerous

White folks who take most or all of the eight considerations seriously. And the high percentage of segregated churches seems to show that this is not likely to happen.

Another possibility is for White churches to deal with these eight considerations—all of them—with training sessions, discussion groups, reading, sermons, and action. White churches that are intentional and persistent about doing so may feel more welcoming to people of color. To be welcoming to people of color, though, it is not enough for individuals in a White church to smile, shake hands, and be friendly toward individual non-White people. Non-White Christians who take seriously any of these eight considerations very probably will still feel uneasy, even though they are glad when White Christians are individually friendly toward them. White Christians must change in most or all of the eight ways for non-White Christians who take those eight considerations seriously to feel fully at home in White churches, or to feel at one with White people who are part of their churches. And that seems unlikely to occur on a large scale in the United States. The eight considerations describe realities that are too deeply entrenched for that to happen.

It might be, of course, that some people of color do not take any of the eight considerations seriously. For them, there would be little racial difficulty in joining with White Christians. No one knows how many people of color are like this, but it probably is not a high number, given the highly racialized culture in the United States. There would not, accordingly, be widespread integration for this reason.

Still another possibility is for people of color who take the eight consideration seriously to set aside their concerns for the sake of Christian unity. This, however, is a nonstarter. It puts the full burden of integration onto people of color. The eight considerations describe realities that have been brought about by White Americans, so to put the burden of integration solely onto non-White people is unjust.

For a fourth possibility, let us return to Howard Thurman's statement quoted above about "a moment when the Roman and the Jew emerged as neither Roman nor Jew, but as two human spirits."[151] Thurman pursues this possibility when he says that "the experience of the common worship of God is such a moment."[152] In this moment, Thurman continues, "the relations of the individual to his God should take priority over conditions of class, race, power, status, wealth, or the like."[153] This description of a common moment of worship reflects Paul's declaration that in Christ "there is no longer Jew or Greek, there is no longer slave or free, there is no longer male and female" (Gal 3:28). Paul is stating in this verse that Christians should regard themselves as one regardless of differences in class, race, power, status, wealth, or educational level. Though Christians differ in these respects, they are not to regard them when they join in one space to worship their common God. Both White and non-White Christians should set aside their racial context when in that one space.

Thurman appears to believe that this fourth option is a real possibility. Though White Americans are "racial enemies" of non-White Americans, people of color are to follow Jesus's command to love their enemies. The burden of integration does not fall just on people of color, though, for White people are to free themselves from their "white necessity."[154] "The ethical demand upon the more privileged and the underprivileged is the same," Thurman states.[155] Both White and non-White Christians are to free themselves from the racial barriers that divide them. For non-White people, he says, this means forgiving White people for the severe injuries that they have inflicted on people of color, and freeing themselves of "the will to retaliation that keeps alive [their] hatred."[156] For White people, it means adopting "the attitude of respect for personality," which will result in a state in which "the heavy weight of status has been sloughed off."[157]

Thurman is not just an idealist, though. He is fully aware that segregation "poisons all normal contacts of those persons involved."[158] Churches in the United States have become "one of the chief instruments for guaranteeing barriers."[159] These barriers are on both sides of the racial divide: White oppression and non-White aversion. The ideal has been shattered on the rocks of racial and class realities. Thurman may have hoped that the ideal would be realized, but that 1949 hope has turned out to be more of an illusory wish.

Frederick Douglass too was skeptical of integration without significant change. In his case, it was the abolition of slavery that was needed. When he was enslaved, he went to the same church that his owner did, sitting up in the gallery with other slaves, but was treated badly during the week, sometimes with whippings.[160] Can you sit under the same church roof on Sunday as someone who whips you on Monday? Or even one who is kind about holding you in bondage?[161] For Douglass, forgiving slaveholders for past wrongs was not enough. The slaveholders had to change as well. It could not be that on the one cruelty-free day of the week you associated with those who were heartlessly dehumanizing and violent toward you the rest of the week.

To those who say that the conditions described in the eight considerations are not nearly as bad as slavery, the reply is that one should listen to American people of color who have been harmed because of those considerations. They have felt otherized, alienated, dehumanized, traumatized, and subordinated because of them. Devlin and Jonathan vividly testify to this.

To those who say that it is unrealistic to expect that all of the eight considerations be undone before Thurman's "being one in Christ" can be achieved, the answer is, "Yes, that may be true." It may be that some Christian people of color will feel welcome in a White church when some of the eight considerations are being seriously addressed. But it would be unrealistic to expect that oneness will exist very extensively in US churches without at least some genuine progress in undoing all or nearly all of the considerations. Non-White churchgoers cannot be expected to associate with White Christians on Sundays without some guarantee that the White Christians are working on racial equity in a variety of ways the rest of the week.

What about Christian hope? Cannot God change human hearts? The answer is that, yes, God can indeed bring it about that enough people change so that church segregation will no longer exist. But the mere possibility of God's doing this is not enough on which to base hope. We often use "hope" to designate an emotion that lies somewhere between expectations and wishes. With expectations, we believe that there is reasonable evidence that an event will occur—"I am expecting that Kendall will be here for our hike. She said she would be coming along." With wishes, we believe that there is good evidence that an event will not occur—"I wish Kendall could go hiking with us today, but she said she has to do something else." With hope, we believe that there is more evidence than there is for wishing but less than there is for expecting—"I hope Kendall can make it to our hike. She said she might be able to come." The same goes for Christian realities— I am expecting to live after I die, I wish that everyone in the United States would adopt the values enunciated in the Sermon on the Mount, and I hope that my friend who is searching for something to believe in will become a Christian. Often, "hope" in Christian contexts is used to refer to each of these, but it would be more accurate to use "expect" and "wish" as well.

Integration of churches strikes me as being in the wishing category— there is good evidence that it will not occur to any great extent. There is, to be sure, good evidence that some individuals, White and non-White, will

Why Church Integration May Never Happen

do what is necessary for racial harmony to occur and that integration will occur in some churches, such as in Lisa's and Devlin's. But there is also good evidence that not enough people will do so for integration to be widely embraced in the United States. Given that US churches have been segregated for the last two centuries, it is likely that they will remain segregated, at least to a great extent. It is, accordingly, appropriate—and desirable—to wish for church integration, but hoping for it seems unfounded, whether or not one is a Christian. One needs some evidence for thinking that God might well bring integration about. Unfortunately, as things currently stand, there does not seem to be good evidence for this.

What about the claim that there is no independent, statistically verifiable evidence—no randomized, double-blind, controlled experiment—that can sort out race from culture, and therefore no basis for saying that segregation in US churches is due more to racialization than culture? This issue is addressed by sociologists, some taking one side and some the other. The point I want to make is that no matter what the sociologists decide, most people of color probably regard at least some of the eight racial considerations as decisive reasons for staying away from White congregations. There is probably no survey that deals with this assertion. But the mere fact that the United States is a highly racialized culture makes the assertion probable.

Two acquaintances have spoken to the issue. When I asked "Caroline," who has an Asian ancestry, whether she would be comfortable being part of a White church, she replied, "Not unless it had race as a priority." On Facebook, a Black acquaintance responded to a tweet by former President Donald Trump on July 29, 2020. Trump's tweet said, "I am happy to inform all of the people living their Suburban Lifestyle Dream that you will no longer be bothered or financially hurt by having low income housing built in your neighborhood. Your housing prices will go up based on the market, and crime will go down. I have rescinded the Obama-Biden AFFH Rule. Enjoy!" The Affirmatively Furthering Fair Housing Rule, adopted in 2015 under President Obama, was designed to ensure fairness for federally protected categories, including race, by requiring a study of the racial composition of a neighborhood before the Federal Housing Authority (FHA) could issue mortgages to people wanting to buy houses in that neighborhood.

My Black acquaintance's response to Trump's tweet was, "This is the reason why people like me, who look like me, will never feel fully at home in the burbs, or fully welcomed in White church spaces, or fully a part of primarily White institutions, or fully a part of America."

The assertions from these two persons of color lend some support to the thesis that non-White Christians will not feel welcome in White spaces, including White churches, without significant changes by White people with regard to race. Those of us who are White should work toward church integration but without illusion about what needs to be done to achieve success.

Devlin

Breaking Down Walls

In Devlin's first story, he described a painful experience he had with a predominantly White church in Illinois. He is now the lead pastor of a racially diverse church in Massachusetts. In this story, he describes how that church has promoted racial harmony, including the breaking down of a literal wall.

FROM DAY ONE, IN 2018, when my wife and I started a church in Massachusetts, we had an outward focus. We wanted, as a church, to take seriously the biblical command to love our neighbors as ourselves. When we asked who our neighbors were, we decided that they were the people in the community where we planted the church. So we became something of a missional church. Those who joined us on Sundays or in our small groups were being equipped to go out and apply the gospel to the social issues of the day, to the common struggles of people everyday. We were pouring out the love of Christ on the pavements of our neighborhoods.

When you have an outward focus, you are already thinking of others first. You automatically ask, "How do I bridge the gap between people who are far from God and God?" The church is that bridge. Individuals in the church make themselves be the bridge between others and the Christ they worship and serve.

If you focus on what is inside the church building, you are centering on the church's programs. You do this and you do that. You are thinking about how to preserve what is within the church. Everything you do in the life of the church happens first in the church body, and then, later, you do outreaches.

We flipped that. For us, everything we do is for our community. I think of myself as the pastor of the city in which the church exists, and I hang out with my friends on Sunday morning and other times we gather.

So, from the church's beginning, we looked at the needs of people. If you start with this, you are putting the *imago Dei*—the image of God—front and center when you think about individuals. You are paying attention to whatever they bring to the table—their baggage, fears, doubts, and frustrations—especially frustrations with the church—as well as their race, sexual orientation, and economic means.

All of this is a foundation for specific programs. We start with the idea that we have to be focused on people outside the church. This reshapes where we begin our conversations and is the model for discipling people in the church. If we have Jesus, this affects how we see others. It moves us to love them as we love ourselves and to set aside our biases, creeds, and supposed conclusions about individuals. It is hard to be self-centered with this foundation.

We have done several specific things that focus on race. When George Floyd was murdered in May of 2020, we created a safe space inside our church to talk about it. We gathered weekly in small, online groups to check in with each other. "How are you doing? How are you feeling about this?"

We African Americans were in mourning. We were hurt. We were in pain. We were telling our sisters and brothers in the church how to respond to us. Other minority groups started to grasp the plight of African Americans in our country compared to how they saw themselves. A White individual understood for the first time what his privilege looked like.

We also started a group that worked through *Be the Bridge: Pursuing God's Heart for Racial Reconciliation* by Latasha Morrison. We invited people who didn't attend our church to be part of the group, and we purchased books for those in it.

In June of 2020, a month after George Floyd's murder, we felt the need for an event where we Black people could smile a little because of the pain we had been in. We put on an outdoor concert that we called Hope Is Rising. We invited community leaders to be part of it, though we sponsored it as a church so that we could proclaim the name of Jesus at it. We sang about Jesus. We sang worship songs. And we had a panel discussion with the mayor, a police officer, and members of a newly formed group called Coalition of Black Residents. Plus, there were bands that played.

We were all encouraged by the concert. Students, teachers, community leaders, and pastors from area churches were involved in it, and so were Black-owned businesses. We had secured a parking lot so that people could stay in their cars because of the pandemic. The concert sold out with 150 cars, the limit for the parking lot. The event was the community coming together to urge us African Americans and our allies to keep going, because we were all feeling very broken and stressed.

In June of the year before, we decided to create a space to talk about hard topics. So we built what we called the Ally Wall, painted it black, and wrote at the bottom, "Take a marker and write the stereotypes that you have believed or that have been placed on you regarding race, gender, sexual orientation, or nationality." We also put cards on the wall for people to take. They said, "To be an Ally is to take on the struggle as your own, stand up even when you feel scared, transfer the benefits of your privilege to those who lack it, and acknowledge that while you too feel pain, the conversation is not always about you." Over the course of a month, as the wall traveled to the churches in the city that we were partnering with, it acquired numerous comments.

Actually, we made two walls, each eight by eight feet square. They were heavy, so we used a U-Haul truck to transport them to the churches. At the end of the month, we took the walls to our church, where we had a Sunday morning gathering of lament and repentance at which we committed ourselves "to rebuilding our diverse and inclusive community on trust, peace, love, and engagement."

At the gathering, we had a panel discussion. A transgender woman, who is a devout Catholic, a Jewish police officer, and I talked about the four issues listed on the walls and the response of US churches to them.

After the discussion, we gave everyone hammers and other instruments of destruction so that they could tear the walls down. That was our symbol to say that we were going to break down barriers that divide us. After we tore the walls down, we had Communion to show that we can all walk together.

It was a powerful moment. Here we were, an evangelical church having a conversation in which a Black man, a Jewish police officer, and a transgender woman talk about social issues and the American church's response.

At the time, I had been preaching on what it meant for Jesus to be an ally. We looked at how he responded to the Samaritan woman and the Samaritans in her town, as described in John 4. When Jesus encountered the woman who was caught in adultery, he protected her. He gave the blind man sight and healed the lame man. Then he told them to go and sin no more. We can't reverse that when Jesus never modeled it that way. He never told people that he wanted them to get right, to get holy, to be saved, to pull themselves together before he would respond to their needs. He put others before himself, and he put his reputation on the line. He didn't make things about himself but about those others and their needs. That is what an ally does.

It is the same for racial harmony. We need to show up. We need to be okay with getting our hands a little dirty. We need to see that loving our neighbors as ourselves is not as simple as we might think. It will affect the way we vote and the way we see ourselves and our organizations and systems. We can't just write statements or make comments or preach from the pulpit about the social climate without actually stepping out of our comfortable churches and stepping into the messes in our society. You can't do racial justice if you are not going to listen to the folks who are affected by injustice. Everyone needs to move, whether that means making a phone call to someone, reading a book, or partnering with a church down the street that is not like ours. Everyone needs to get uncomfortable.

14

What We Whites Must Do

FLOATING AROUND ONLINE IS a post titled "75 Things White People Can Do for Racial Justice." Another post has the number as ninety-seven, and still another has it as a hundred. One of the things in the hundred post is to contact your local town council to see what policies it has in place to address police violence. Another is to call or write your state legislator to ask that racial impact studies be done for bills dealing with criminal justice.

Without detracting from the importance of these action lists, I want to offer a different list, one that deals with moral character instead of specific actions that we White people can take. The items on the list are not just ones that *can* be taken, but ones that *must* be taken if racial equity is to be addressed. The six items on the list are based on themes in this book. Together they identify the character traits White people must have to regard racial equity as a priority.

1. Openness to learning about the trauma people of color have experienced
2. Empathy toward the trauma people of color have experienced
3. Willingness to uproot the sense of White superiority
4. Valuing a fair apportionment of power for people of color
5. A proclivity to employ the Golden Rule in racial contexts

6. Having right moral perception of non-White people—the same respect and care that one expects others to have toward oneself

Each of these is associated with a virtue. Openness is the virtue of being welcoming. We can picture the stance of openness by imagining a person whose forearms are extended in front of her, elbows at her side, with palms facing up and hands open wide. This is the picture of one who gladly receives others into her life. She listens to the delights and the traumas of those others. She attends to their concerns and is present with them when they rejoice and when they cry. They feel safe telling her about their deep concerns.

It is a short step from being open to being empathetic, though it is not automatic. An empathetic person is not only open to learning about the traumas of others; she is sensitive and responsive to them. She expresses that response on her face and in her bodily comportment, along with appropriate words. Though not actually having the feelings and emotions of others, she experiences joy and pain when those others convey their joyful and painful feelings to her.

The person who values racial equity is aware of the common human impulse to think of oneself as superior to others, and she roots around in her inner terrain to discover how she herself has succumbed to it. Her aim is to resist the impulse. Though she acknowledges that she has the impulse, she also desires to regard herself as equal to those who are racially different. She does not regard people who look like her as normal humans and people of other races as less than human. Everyone, she feels, is a normal human.

The person who values racial equity is also aware of the common human impulse to take more than one's fair share of power, authority, advantage, and control. Though she recognizes that she too has the impulse, she combats it. She laments having acquired more than her fair share of advantage and power because of being White. Her desire for fairness prompts her to use that advantage so as to secure equal opportunities for others regardless of race. She is willing to advocate for equal opportunities and equal rights even though that means she herself may have to give up some of the undue advantage she has accrued by being White.

In a way, being imaginative in racial ways underlies the previous four virtues. One needs to be imaginative to appreciate the trauma American people of color have experienced and to have empathy toward them. One cannot be aware of one's own sense of superiority or the White advantages one has enjoyed without picturing to oneself what it is like not to have these.

What We Whites Must Do

Last, one's moral perception of people of color is shaped by these five virtues so as to produce the same respect and care for them that one expects others to have toward oneself. A moral perception of someone is based on a moral assessment of them. Each of the five virtues presupposes an equal moral assessment of non-White and White people. Accordingly, with these virtues, a White person will have right moral perceptions of non-White and White people and thus will have equal respect and care for both.

I want now to connect the acquisition of these six character traits to several of James Baldwin's statements I quoted earlier. He declares that "we cannot be free until they are free."[162] He presupposes in this that White people are not free: "They have had to believe for many years, and for innumerable reasons that black men are inferior to white men."[163] In fact, Baldwin says, "They [White people] are trapped."[164] The absolutely important thing about acquiring the six character traits is that they free those of us who are White. They free us from having closed ourselves to the experiences of people of color and from not understanding those experiences. They free us from the deep psychological need to feel superior to people of color, a need that has us tightly in its grip. They free us from collectively hanging on to the advantages we have inherited and from the belief that non-White equity is prejudicial to White rights. They free us from unwillingness to have equal respect and care toward non-White people. Acquiring the six character traits is liberating to White people.

It is also liberating to people of color, though in a different way. To call for the adoption of these character traits in a highly racialized culture—one in which Whiteness is widespread—is to call for a racial revolution. It is a revolution of character, but it is also a revolution of action. Character traits, to be genuine, must be accompanied by dispositions to act in accordance with the traits. A generous person has a disposition to be generous when relevant occasions present themselves, and a kind person has a disposition to act kindly when in a circumstance in which one can be kind. It is the same for the six character traits. One who has them will have the disposition, and thus the tendency, to act in accordance with them. If enough White people in the highly racialized culture of the United States were to adopt the six character traits, non-White equity would become a living reality and non-White people would be liberated from the racial disparities that have afflicted them for four hundred years.

This last statement needs to be qualified, for institutions—businesses, governments, and churches—also need to adopt the six character traits for racial equity to come alive and for non-White folks to be liberated. It may sound odd to say that institutions can have character traits. Here is how to make sense of the idea. When you go to your bank to make a withdrawal, you don't say that Veronica Lopez, the teller, gives you money. You say that the bank gives you money. Ms. Lopez is acting in accordance with the policies and practices of the bank, and because she does you say that it is the bank and not Ms. Lopez from which you get your money.

Now suppose Ms. Lopez is a loan officer who operates in accordance with racist loan policies. In this case, you would say that the bank is acting in racist ways. And when it does, it has the character trait of being racist. If, however, it were a policy and practice of the bank to act in accordance with virtues associated with the six character traits, then the bank would no longer be acting in racist ways. Individuals who work at the bank would be acting in conformity with the nonracist policies and practices of the bank, and in doing so their actions would be official actions of the bank. However, if those individuals were to go home and act in accordance with the virtues associated with the six character traits, it would be they themselves, as individuals, who have the virtues and traits.

Institutions, in addition to individuals, need to adopt the virtues associated with the six character traits to make racial equity come alive, because it could be that individuals act in accordance with the virtues, as individuals, but institutions do not. In this case, there would still be a good deal of racism in one's culture. There would be individuals who act in accordance with the six virtues as individuals but not in their official capacity in institutions. They would be split people—"double-minded," to use James's word (Jas 1:8). Presumably, enough of them would be aware of that split and find it so intolerable that they would exert pressure on the institutions of which they are a part to change their racist policies and practices. In this way, there is a connection between individuals and institutions—the former can influence the latter to change. The latter can also influence the former to change. So both individuals and institutions need to acquire the six virtues. If enough of them do so in a highly racialized culture, that culture will change radically. Given that US culture is highly racialized, adopting the six virtues will produce that radical change. If the change does not occur, it will be because not enough individuals and institutions have adopted the six virtues.

Endnotes

1. Hart, *Trouble I've Seen*, 23–25.
2. Yancy, *Look, a White!*, 154.
3. The books students read were *Thinking about Race* by Naomi Zack; *Race Matters* by Cornel West; *The Color of Our Shame: Race and Justice in Our Time* by Christopher J. Lebron; *Christian Faith and Social Justice: Five Views*, edited by Vic McCracken; and *Affirmative Action: Social Justice or Unfair Preference?* by Albert G. Mosley and Nicholas Capaldi; and part of *Look, a White!* by George Yancy. Students also read online articles, including "White Fragility" by Robin DiAngelo; "White Privilege: Unpacking the Invisible Knapsack" by Peggy McIntosh; and "Playfulness, 'World'-Traveling, and Loving Perception" by María Lugones. The television series students watched is titled *The African Americans: Many Rivers to Cross*, narrated by Henry Louis Gates Jr., director of the Hutchins Center for African American Studies at Harvard University.
4. Baldwin, "Dungeon," 8.
5. Baldwin, "Dungeon," 9.
6. These statistics appear in Nesbit, "Institutional Racism." See chapter 7 for more statistics on racial disparities.
7. The book that exhaustively describes racially injurious governmental laws and policies regarding segregation is Rothstein, *Color of Law*. See pages 64–57, 81–83, and 127–31 for the instances described.
8. Sue, "Racial Microaggressions."
9. Hart, *Trouble I've Seen*, 21.
10. Hart, *Trouble I've Seen*, 21.
11. DiAngelo, *White Fragility*, 9.
12. Lugones, "Playfulness," 3–19.
13. Baldwin, "Dungeon," 9–10.
14. Baldwin, "Dungeon," 10.
15. Emerson and Smith, *Divided by Faith*. See chapter 6, "Let's Be Friends," 115–33.
16. DiAngelo, *White Fragility*, 5.

Endnotes

17. Wise, *White Like Me*, 133.
18. Wise, *White Like Me*, 133.
19. Wise, *White Like Me*, 134.
20. Wise, *White Like Me*, 134.
21. Yancy, *Look, a White!*, 22.
22. Yancy, *Look, a White!*, 25.
23. Yancy, *Look, a White!*, 163, 159.
24. Yancy, *Look, a White!*, 168.
25. Yancy, *Look, a White!*, 173.
26. Yancy, *Look, a White!*, 168.
27. Yancy, *Look, a White!*, 169.
28. For an extended discussion of this elevator instance from the perspective of both a Black and White person, see chapter 2, "The Elevator Effect," in Yancy, *Black Bodies, White Gazes*, 17–49.
29. Hannah-Jones, "Black America Fears the Police."
30. Baldwin, "My Dungeon Shook," 8–9.
31. Baldwin, "My Dungeon Shook," 8.
32. Baldwin, "My Dungeon Shook," 9.
33. Baldwin, "My Dungeon Shook," 9.
34. Baldwin, "James Baldwin Interviewed." Transcript in Yancy, *Backlash*, 54.
35. Rothstein, *Color of Law*, 196–97.
36. Rothstein, *Color of Law*, 197, 230, 197.
37. Baggett, "Eugene 'Bull' Connor."
38. I had, in fact, done this in 1988 for twenty-six hours on the streets of Chicago: see "Homeless for a Day," at www.cliffordwilliams.net/homelessforaday.
39. Quoted in Yancy, *Black Bodies, White Gazes*, 36. For the actual testimony, see Linder, "Excerpts." The testimony from one of the officers about the downed King includes these statements: "He grimaced, he kinda gave out like a bear like yell." "He repeated this ah this ah groan similar to like a wounded animal and then he ah I could see the vibrations on him but he seem to be overcoming it."
40. Both quotes are from Lebron, *Color of Our Shame*, 146.
41. Lebron, *Color of Our Shame*, 4–5, 44, 50.
42. Feagin, *White Racial Frame*, 104, quoted in Yancy, *Backlash*, 48.
43. Dixon and Telles, "Skin Color and Colorism."
44. At policingequity.org.
45. "Changing Attitudes by Changing Behavior."
46. Ligon, "'Turn This Town Out.'"
47. Azikiwe, "Stokely Carmichael."
48. Recounted in more detail in my "Singing at an Anti-KKK Protest," at www.cliffordwilliams.net/singing.
49. Azikiwe, "Stokely Carmichael."
50. Ture and Hamilton, *Black Power*, 46.
51. Ture and Hamilton, *Black Power*, 46, 47.
52. Ture and Hamilton, *Black Power*, 47.
53. Ture and Hamilton, *Black Power*, 47.
54. Ture and Hamilton, *Black Power*, 47.
55. Smith, *Less than Human*, 119.
56. Baldwin, "Dungeon," 8–9.

Endnotes

57. Baldwin, "Dungeon," 9
58. Baldwin, "Dungeon," 9.
59. Ture and Hamilton, *Black Power*, 46.
60. Mathews, *At the Altar of Lynching*, 26, 27.
61. "The reality of whiteness, however, expresses itself in the form of a conglomerate set of interlocking forces. These forces inhabit every nook and cranny of American life, possessing the power to make themselves representative." Yancy, *Black Bodies, White Gazes*, 179.
62. Brown, *I'm Still Here*, 106.
63. Johnson, "Racial Inequality."
64. Lockhart, "New Report." The new report is Blake and Epstein, "Listening to Black Women." The article Lockhart refers to about the increasing use of discipline is Rhor, "Criminalization of Black Girls."
65. *Pushout*.
66. English et al., "Racial Discrimination."
67. Death Penalty Information Numbers, "Race and the Death Penalty."
68. Drug Policy Alliance, "Drug War."
69. Weir, "Inequality at School."
70. Ford, "Homeownership."
71. Department of Housing and Urban Development, "HUD Charges Facebook."
72. Gramlich, "Gap."
73. Equal Justice Initiative, "Illegal Racial Discrimination."
74. Weeks, "Fairness in the Exceptions."
75. Edwards, Lee, and Esposito, "Risk of Being Killed."
76. Centers for Disease Control, *National Vital Statistics Report*.
77. Centers for Disease Control, "Pregnancy-Related Deaths."
78. Neighmond, "Racial Gaps." The investigative report is Martin and Montagne, "Black Mothers Keep Dying."
79. Martin and Montagne, "Black Mothers Keep Dying."
80. Ghandnoosh, "Race and Punishment."
81. Ford, "Homeownership."
82. Bridges, "Implicit Bias."
83. Ledford, "Millions of Black People Affected."
84. Bertrand and Sendhil, "Are Emily and Greg More Employable?"
85. Ghandnoosh, "Race and Punishment."
86. Horowitz, Brown, and Cox, "Role of Race."
87. Williams, "Study Supports Suspicion." See Center for Policing Equity at policingequity.org.
88. Moore, "Being a Protective Black Mom."
89. US Department of Education, "Data Highlights on School Climate."
90. Camera, "White Students." The EdBuild report is "NonWhite School Districts Get $23 Billion Less."
91. *Toxic Wastes and Race at Twenty*.
92. Mohai and Saha, "Which Came First?"
93. Ortiz, "Inside 100 Million Police Traffic Stops." The Stanford Open Policing Project is at openpolicing.stanford.edu. See Sorin and Burns, "Driving While Black," for vivid depictions of traffic stops.
94. Fletcher, "Stop."

Endnotes

95. Ramey, "America's Unfair Rules."
96. US Bureau of Labor Statistics, "Labor Force Characteristics."
97. Maxwell and Root, "Five Truths."
98. Hegewisch and Hartmann, "Gender Wage Gap."
99. Luhby, "Wealth Inequality."
100. Holland, "Average Black Family."
101. Chiles, "Black Ministry Students at Duke."
102. Workneh, "Two Trailblazers."
103. "Your Stories of Racism."
104. Burch, "Gardening while Black."
105. Jones, "Growing Up Black."
106. Simon, "Racism in Schools."
107. Kambhampaty, "'I Will Not Stand Silent.'"
108. An, "Naperville Schools." Griggs, "Living while Black," lists links to reports about everyday activities of Black Americans for which police were called during 2018, including taking a phone call while in a hotel lobby, operating a lemonade store, waiting for a friend at Starbucks, barbecuing at a park, working out at a gym, moving into an apartment, napping in a university common room, asking for directions, helping a homeless man, delivering newspapers, working as a firefighter, swimming in a pool, and many more.
109. Yancy, *Black Bodies, White Gazes*, 223.
110. Okeowo, "History of Black Life."
111. A different argument against abortion does not rest on the claim that the fetus is a person beginning with conception. It asserts that abortion is wrong for the same reason that killing an adult is wrong, namely, because it deprives the fetus of a future filled with intrinsically good experiences. Those who adopt this approach believe that abortion is as seriously wrong as those who adopt the fetus-is-a-person approach. See Marquis, "Why Abortion Is Immoral."
112. Neighmond, "Racial Gaps." See also Villarosa, "America's Black Mothers."
113. Bridges, "Implicit Bias."
114. Ledford, "Racial Bias in Health-Care Algorithms."
115. Equal Justice Initiative, "Illegal Racial Discrimination."
116. Centers for Disease Control, "Abortion, Data and Statistics."
117. Equal Justice Initiative, "Lynching in America."
118. See Mathews, *At the Altar of Lynching*.
119. West, *Race Matters*, 22–23.
120. Sue, "Racial Microaggressions."
121. Sue, "Racial Microaggressions."
122. Sue, "Racial Microaggressions."
123. Sue, "Racial Microaggressions."
124. Lopez, "Ta-Nehisi Coates."
125. For other accounts of how it feels to be called an Oreo, see Pierre, "How It Feels"; and Colon, "Please Don't Call Me an Oreo."
126. McIntosh, "Whiteness."
127. Sue, "Racial Microaggressions."
128. "Then it dawned upon me with a certain suddenness that I was different from the others; . . . shut out from their world by a vast veil." DuBois, *Souls*, 2.
129. West, *Race Matters*, 19.

Endnotes

130. Lebron, *Color of Our Shame*, 104, 109–14.
131. Smith, *Less than Human*, 103–31.
132. Arsenault, *Freedom Riders*. See the documentary *Freedom Riders* for vivid depictions of the violence directed toward the riders.
133. Arsenault, *Freedom Riders*, 478.
134. Arsenault, *Freedom Riders*, 140–46.
135. Arsenault, *Freedom Riders*, 153–60.
136. Arsenault, *Freedom Riders*, 212.
137. Arsenault, *Freedom Riders*, 213–14.
138. Arsenault, *Freedom Riders*, 430.
139. Douglass, "West India Emancipation."
140. Baldwin, "My Dungeon Shook," 9.
141. Baldwin, "My Dungeon Shook," 9.
142. Horowitz, "Most Americans."
143. Northup, *Twelve Years a Slave*, 113.
144. Jacobs, *Incidents in the Life of a Slave Girl*, 517–18.
145. Thurman, *Jesus and the Disinherited*, 85.
146. Thurman, *Jesus and the Disinherited*, 85–86.
147. Thurman, *Jesus and the Disinherited*, 87.
148. Emerson and Smith, *Divided by Faith*. See especially chapter 5, "Controlling One's Own Destiny," and chapter 8, "Structurally Speaking."
149. See Briggs, "Multiracial Churches"; and Gjelten, "Multiracial Congregations."
150. Emerson and Smith, *Divided by Faith*, 158.
151. Thurman, *Jesus and the Disinherited*, 85.
152. Thurman, *Jesus and the Disinherited*, 88.
153. Thurman, *Jesus and the Disinherited*, 88.
154. Thurman, *Jesus and the Disinherited*, 90.
155. Thurman, *Jesus and the Disinherited*, 96.
156. Thurman, *Jesus and the Disinherited*, 97.
157. Thurman, *Jesus and the Disinherited*, 92, 94.
158. Thurman, *Jesus and the Disinherited*, 88.
159. Thurman, *Jesus and the Disinherited*, 88.
160. Blight, *Frederick Douglass*, 115.
161. "The slaveholder, kind or cruel, . . . is . . . every hour silently whetting the knife of vengeance for his own throat." Douglass, quoted in Blight, *Frederick Douglass*, 262.
162. Baldwin, "My Dungeon Shook," 10.
163. Baldwin, "My Dungeon Shook," 8–9.
164. Baldwin, "My Dungeon Shook," 8.

Bibliography

An, Susie. "Naperville Schools Try to Rebuild Trust after Incident Exposes Persistent Race Issues." National Public Radio: WBEZ Chicago, December 10, 2019. https://www.npr.org/local/309/2019/12/10/786696510/naperville-schools-try-to-rebuild-trust-after-incident-exposes-persistent-race-issues.

Arsenault, Raymond. *Freedom Riders: 1961 and the Struggle for Racial Justice*. New York: Oxford University Press, 2006.

Azikiwe, Abayomi. "Stokely Carmichael, Black Power and the Age of Political Repression." *Pambazuka News*, June 16, 2016. https://www.pambazuka.org/pan-africanism/stokely-carmichael-black-power-and-age-political-repression.

Baggett, James L. "Eugene 'Bull' Connor." *Encyclopedia of Alabama*, August 15, 2012. http://encyclopediaofalabama.org/article/h-1091.

Baldwin, James. "James Baldwin Interviewed by Kenneth Clark." May 24, 1963. https://www.youtube.com/watch?v==Ua2Rb7vVsMY. Transcription in Yancy, *Backlash*, 54.

———. "My Dungeon Shook: Letter to My Nephew on the One Hundredth Anniversary of Emancipation." In *The Fire Next Time*, 1–10. New York: Vintage, 1993. First published in *The Progressive*, December 1, 1962. https://progressive.org/magazine/letter-nephew/.

Bertrand, Marianne, and Sendhil Mullainathan. "Are Emily and Greg More Employable than Lakisha and Jamal?: A Field Experiment on Labor Market Discrimination." National Bureau of Economic Research, Working Paper 9873, July 2003. https://www.nber.org/papers/w9873.

Blake, Jamilia J., and Rebecca Epstein. "Listening to Black Women and Girls: Lived Experiences of Adultification Bias." Georgetown Law Center on Poverty and Inequality, May 11, 2019. https://www.law.georgetown.edu/poverty-inequality-center/wp-content/uploads/sites/14/2019/05/Listening-to-Black-Women-and-Girls.pdf.

Blight, David W. *Frederick Douglass: Prophet of Freedom*. New York: Simon & Schuster, 2018.

Bibliography

Bridges, Khiara M. "Implicit Bias and Racial Disparities in Health Care." *Human Rights Magazine*, August 1, 2018. https://www.americanbar.org/groups/crsj/publications/human_rights_magazine_home/the-state-of-healthcare-in-the-united-states/racial-disparities-in-health-care/.

Briggs, David. "In Multiracial Churches, Pastors of Color Hitting 'The Same White Wall.'" *Ahead of the Trend* (blog), Association of Religion Data Archives, February 27, 2019. http://blogs.thearda.com/trend/featured/in-multiracial-churches-pastors-of-color-hitting-the-same-white-wall/.

Brown, Austin Channing. *I'm Still Here: Black Dignity in a World Made for Whiteness*. New York: Convergent, 2018.

Burch, Audra D. S. "How 'Gardening while Black' Almost Landed This Detroit Man in Jail." *New York Times*, October 26, 2018. https://www.nytimes.com/2018/10/26/us/white-women-calling-police-black-men.html.

Camera, Lauren. "White Students Get More K-12 Funding than Students of Color: Report." *U.S. News and World Report*, February 26, 2019. https://www.usnews.com/news/education-news/articles/2019-12-26/white-students-get-more-k-12-funding-than-students-of-color-report.

Centers for Disease Control. "Abortion, Data and Statistics." Reproductive Health. https://www.cdc.gov/reproductivehealth/data_stats/abortion.htm.

———. *National Vital Statistics Report* 68:9 (June 24, 2019). https://www.cdc.gov/nchs/data/nvsr/nvsr68/nvsr68_09_tables-508.pdf.

———. "*Vital Signs*: Pregnancy-Related Deaths, United States, 2011–2015, and Strategies for Prevention, 13 States, 2013–2017." Morbidity and Mortality Weekly Report, May 10, 2019. https://www.cdc.gov/mmwr/volumes/68/wr/mm6818e1.htm.

"Changing Attitudes by Changing Behavior." Ch. 5.3 in *Principles of Social Psychology*. Twin Cities, MN: University of Minnesota Libraries Publishing, 2010. Author's name and original publisher removed. https://open.lib.umn.edu/socialpsychology/chapter/5-3-changing-attitudes-by-changing-behavior/.

Chiles, Nick. "Black Ministry Students at Duke Say They Face Unequal Treatment and Racism." National Public Radio: WBEZ Chicago, May 24, 2017. https://www.wlrn.org/2017-15-24/black-ministry-students-at-duke-say-they-face-unequal-treatment-and-racism.

Colon, Nia. "Please Don't Call Me an Oreo, or a White Girl for That Matter." *Thought Catalog*, January 18, 2015. https://thoughtcatalog.com/nia-colon/2015/01/please-dont-call-me-an-oreo-or-a-white-girl-for-that-matter/.

Death Penalty Information Numbers. "Race and the Death Penalty by the Numbers." June 5, 2021. https://deathpenaltyinfo.org/policy-issues/race/race-and-the-death-penalty-by-the-numbers.

Department of Housing and Urban Development. "HUD Charges Facebook with Housing Discrimination over Company's Targeted Advertising Practices." March 28, 2019. https://archives.hud.gov/news/2019/pr19-35.cfm.

DiAngelo, Robin. *White Fragility: Why It's So Hard for White People to Talk about Racism*. Boston: Beacon, 2018.

Dixon, Angela R., and Edward E. Telles. "Skin Color and Colorism: Global Research, Concepts, and Measurement." *Annual Review of Sociology* 43 (May 19, 2017) 405–24. https://www.annualreviews.org/doi/abs/10.1146/annurev-soc-060116-53315?journalCode=soc.

Bibliography

Douglass, Frederick. "West India Emancipation." In *Two Speeches by Frederick Douglass*. Rochester, NY: O. P. Dewey, 1857. https://www.loc.gov/resource/mfd.21039/.

Drug Policy Alliance. "The Drug War, Mass Incarceration and Race." January 2018. https://drugpolicy.org/sites/default/files/drug-war-mass-incarceration-and-race_01_18_0.pdf.

DuBois, W. E. B. *The Souls of Black Folks*. New York: Dover, 1994.

EdBuild. "NonWhite School Districts Get $23 Billion Less than White Districts Despite Serving the Same Number of Students." February, 2019. https://edbuild.org/content/23-billion.

Edwards, Frank, Hedwig Lee, and Michael Esposito. "Risk of Being Killed by Police Use of Force in the United States by Age, Race-Ethnicity, and Sex." *Proceedings of the National Academy of Sciences* 116:34 (August 20, 2019). https://www.pnas.org/content/116/34/16793/tab-figures-data.

Emerson, Michael O., and Christian Smith. *Divided by Faith: Evangelical Religion and the Problem of Race in America*. New York: Oxford University Press, 2000.

English, Devin, et al. "Daily Multidimensional Racial Discrimination among Black U.S. American Adolescents." *Journal of Applied Developmental Psychology* 66 (January–February 2020). https://www.sciencedirect.com/science/article/abs/pii/S0193397319300462.

Equal Justice Initiative. "Illegal Racial Discrimination in Jury Selection: A Continuing Legacy." August 2010. https://eji.org/wp-content/uploads/2019/10/illegal-racial-discrimination-in-jury-selection.pdf.

———. "Lynching in America: Confronting the Legacy of Racial Terror." 3rd ed. 2017. https://eji.org/reports/lynching-in-america/.

Feagin, Joe. *The White Racial Frame: Centuries of Racial Framing and Counter-Framing*. New York: Routledge, 2010.

Fletcher, Michael A. "The Stop: Racial Profiling of Drivers Leaves Legacy of Anger and Fear." *The Undefeated*, May 12, 2018. https://theundefeated.com/features/the-stop-national-geographic-anquan-boldin-racial-profiling-of-drivers-leaves-legacy-of-anger/.

Ford, Carmel. "Homeownership by Race and Ethnicity." *Eye on Housing*, National Association of Home Builders, December 15, 2017. https://eyeonhousing.org/2017/12/homeownership-by-race-and-ethnicity/.

Freedom Riders. American Experience. Public Broadcasting System and Firelight Media, first aired May 16, 2011. https://www.pbs.org/wgbh/americanexperience/films/freedomriders/.

German, Lopez. "Ta-Nehisi Coates Has an Incredibly Clear Explanation for Why White People Shouldn't Use the N-Word." *Vox*, November 9, 2017. https://www.vox.com/identities/2017/11/9/16627900/ta-nehisi-coates-n-word.

Ghandnoosh, Nazgol. "Race and Punishment: Racial Perceptions of Crime and Support for Punitive Policies." The Sentencing Project, September 3, 2014. https://www.sentencingproject.org/publications/race-and-punishment-racial-perceptions-of-crime-and-support-for-punitive-policies/.

Gjelten, Tom. "Multiracial Congregations May Not Bridge Racial Divide." National Public Radio, July 17, 2020. https://www.npr.org/2020/07/17/891600067/multiracial-congregations-may-not-bridge-racial-divide.

Gramlich, John. "The Gap between the Number of Blacks and Whites in Prison Is Shrinking." Pew Research Center, April 30, 2019. https://www.pewresearch.org/fact-tank/2019/04/30/shrinking-gap-between-number-of-blacks-and-whites-in-prison/.

Bibliography

Griggs, Brandon. "Living while Black: Here Are All the Routine Activities for Which Police Were Called on African-Americans This Year." *CNN*, December 28, 2018. https://www.cnn.com/2018/12/20/us/living-while-black-police-calls-trnd/index.html.

Hannah-Jones, Nikole. "Yes, Black America Fears the Police. Here's Why." *ProPublica*, March 4, 2015. https://www.propublica.org/article/yes-black-america-fears-the-police-heres-why.

Hart, Drew. *Trouble I've Seen: Changing the Way the Church Views Racism*. Harrisonburg, VA: Herald, 2016.

Hegewisch, Ariane, and Heidi Hartmann. "The Gender Wage Gap: 2018 Earnings Differences by Race and Ethnicity." Institute for Women's Policy Research, March 7, 2019. https://iwpr.org/iwpr-general/the-gender-wage-gap-2018-earnings-differences-by-race-and-ethnicity/.

Holland, Joshua. "The Average Black Family Would Need 228 Years to Build to Wealth of a White Family Today." *The Nation*, August 8, 2016. https://www.thenation.com/article/archive/the-average-black-family-would-need-228-years-to-build-the-wealth-of-a-white-family-today/.

Horowitz, Juliana Menasce. "Most Americans Say the Legacy of Slavery Still Affects Black People in the U.S. Today." Pew Research Center, June 17, 2019. https://www.pewresearch.org/fact-tank/2019/06/17/most-americans-say-the-legacy-of-slavery-still-affects-black-people-in-the-u-s-today/.

Horowitz, Juliana Menasce, Anna Brown, and Kiana Cox. "The Role of Race and Ethnicity in Americans' Personal Lives." Pew Research Center, April 9, 2019. https://www.pewresearch.org/social-trends/2019/04/09/the-role-of-race-and-ethnicity-in-americans-personal-lives/.

Jacobs, Harriet. *Incidents in the Life of a Slave Girl*. In *The Classic Slave Narratives*, edited by Henry Louis Gates Jr. New York: Signet, 2002. First published under Linda Brent, Boston, 1861.

Johnson, Elin. "Racial Inequality, at College and in the Workplace." *Inside Higher Ed.*, October 18, 2019. https://www.insidehighered.com/news/2019/10/18/racial-inequality-college-and-workplace.

Jones, Brian. "Growing Up Black in America: Here's My Story of Everyday Racism." *The Guardian*, June 6, 2018. https://www.theguardian.com/us-news/2018/jun/06/growing-up-black-in-america-racism-education.

Kambhampaty, Anna Purna. "'I Will Not Stand Silent': 10 Asian Americans Reflect on Racism during the Pandemic and the Need for Equality." *Time*, June 25, 2020. https://time.com/5858649/racism-coronavirus/.

Lebron, Christopher J. *The Color of Our Shame: Race and Justice in Our Time*. New York: Oxford University Press, 2013.

Ledford, Heidi. "Millions of Black People Affected by Racial Bias in Health-Care Algorithms." *Nature*, October 26, 2019. https://www.nature.com/articles/d41586-19-03228-26.

Ligon, Tina L. "'Turn This Town Out': Stokely Carmichael, Black Power, and the March Against Fear." *Rediscovering Black History* (blog), National Archives, June 7, 2016. https://rediscovering-black-history.blogs.archives.gov/2016/06/07/turn-this-town-out-stokely-carmichael-black-power-and-the-march-against-fear/.

Linder, Douglas O. "Excerpts from the LAPD Officers' Trial." *Famous Trials* (blog), n.d. https://www.famous-trials.com/lapd/581-excerpts.

Bibliography

Lockhart, P. R. "A New Report Shows How Racism and Bias Deny Black Girls Their Childhoods." *Vox*, May 16, 2019. https://www.vox.com/identities/2019/5/16/18624683/black-girls-racism-bias-adultification-discipline-georgetown.

Lugones, María. "Playfulness, 'World'-Traveling, and Loving Perception." *Hypatia* 2 (1987) 3–19. http://www.iheal.univ-paris3.fr/sites/www.iheal.univ-paris3.fr/files/playfulness.pdf.

Luhby, Tami. "Wealth Inequality Between Blacks and Whites Worsens." *CNN Business*, February 27, 2013. https://money.cnn.com/2013/02/27/news/economy/wealth-whites-blacks/index.html

Marquis, Don. "Why Abortion Is Immoral." *Journal of Philosophy* 86 (1989) 183–202.

Martin, Nina, and Renee Montagne. "Black Mothers Keep Dying after Giving Birth. Shalon Irving's Story Explains Why." National Public Radio, December 7, 2017. https://www.npr.org/2017/12/07/568948782/black-mothers-keep-dying-after-giving-birth-shalon-irvings-story-explains-why.

Mathews, Donald G. *At the Altar of Lynching: Burning Sam Hose in the American South*. New York: Cambridge University Press, 2018.

Maxwell, Connor, and Danielle Root. "Five Truths about Voter Suppression." Center for American Progress, May 12, 2017. https://www.americanprogress.org/issues/race/news/2017/05/12/432339/five-truths-voter-suppression/.

McIntosh, Peggy. "Whiteness: Unpacking the Invisible Knapsack." *Peace and Freedom*, July/August, 1989. https://psychology.umbc.edu/files/2016/10/White-Privilege_McIntosh-1989.pdf.

Mohai, Paul, and Robin Saha. "Which Came First, People or Pollution?: Assessing the Disparate Siting and Post-Siting Demographic Change Hypotheses of Environmental Injustice." *Environmental Research Letters*, November 18, 2015. https://iopscience.iop.org/article/10.1088/1748-9326/10/11/115008/meta.

Moore, Dasia. "Being a Protective Black Mom Isn't a Parenting Choice—It's the Only Choice." *Quartz*, December 20, 2019. https://dasia5.rssing.com/chan-75807505/article19.html.

Neighmond, Patti. "Why Racial Gaps in Maternal Mortality Persist." Connecticut Public Radio, May 25, 2019. https://www.wnpr.org/post/why-racial-gaps-maternal-mortality-persist.

Nesbit, Jeff. "Institutional Racism Is Our Way of Life." *U.S. News and World Report*, May 6, 2015. https://www.usnews.com/news/blogs/at-the-edge/2015/05/06/institutional-racism-is-our-way-of-life.

Northup, Solomon. *Twelve Years a Slave*. Los Angeles: GrayMalkin, 2014. First published by Derby and Miller, 1853.

Okeowo, Alexis. "How Saidiya Hartman Retells the History of Black Life." *The New Yorker*, October 19, 2020. https://www.newyorker.com/magazine/2020/10/26/how-saidiya-hartman-retells-the-history-of-black-life.

Ortiz, Erik. "Inside 100 Million Police Traffic Stops: New Evidence of Racial Bias." *NBC News*, March 13, 2019. https://www.nbcnews.com/news/us-news/inside-100-million-police-traffic-stops-new-evidence-racial-bias-n980556.

Pierre, Ella. "How It Feels When Your Friend Calls You an Oreo." *Blavity*, February 23, 2015. https://blavity.com/feels-friend-calls-oreo?category1=race-identity&category2=opinion.

Pushout: The Criminalization of Black Girls in Schools. https://pushoutfilm.com.

Bibliography

Ramey, Corinne. "America's Unfair Rules of the Road: How Our Transportation System Discriminates against the Most Vulnerable." *Slate*, February 27, 2015. https://slate.com/news-and-politics/2015/02/americas-transportation-system-discriminates-against-minorities-and-poor-federal-funding-for-roads-buses-and-mass-transit-still-segregates-americans.html.

Rhor, Monica. "What Can Be Done to Stop the Criminalization of Black Girls? Rebuild the System." *USA Today*, May 14, 2019. https://www.usatoday.com/in-depth/news/2019/05/14/black-girls-school-discipline-racism-disparities-pushout-solutions/1121061001/.

Rothstein, Richard. *The Color of Law: A Forgotten History of How Our Government Segregated America*. New York: Liveright, 2017.

Simon, Scott, and Samantha Balaban. "How Racism Has Manifested Itself in Schools, as Recalled by Listeners." National Public Radio: WBEZ Chicago, February 9, 2019. https://www.wwno.org/2019-12-09/listeners-share-stories-of-racism-at-school.

Smith, David Livingstone. *Less than Human: Why We Demean, Enslave, and Exterminate Others*. New York: St. Martin's, 2011.

Sorin, Gretchen, and Ric Burns, "Driving While Black: Race, Space, and Mobility in America." Public Broadcasting System, 2020. https://www.pbs.org/video/driving-while-black-race-space-and-mobility-in-america-achvfr/.

Sue, Derald Wing. "Racial Microaggressions in Everyday Life." *Psychology Today*, October 5, 2010. https://www.psychologytoday.com/us/blog/microaggressions-in-everyday-life/201010/racial-microaggressions-in-everyday-life.

Thurman, Howard. *Jesus and the Disinherited*. Boston: Beacon, 1976. First published by Abingdon, 1949.

Toxic Wastes and Race at Twenty: 1987–2007. A Report Prepared for the United Church of Christ Justice & Witness Ministries. United Church of Christ, March 2007. https://issuu.com/theejcc/docs/toxic20.

Ture, Kwame, and Charles V. Hamilton. *Black Power: The Politics of Liberation*. New York: Vintage, 1992. Originally published by Random House, 1967.

US Bureau of Labor Statistics. "Labor Force Characteristics by Race and Ethnicity, 2018." *BLS Reports* 1082 (October 2019). https://www.bls.gov/opub/reports/race-and-ethnicity/2018/home.htm.

US Department of Education, Office for Civil Rights. "School Climate and Safety: Data Highlights on School Climate and Safety in Our Nation's Public Schools, 2015–2016 Civil Rights Data Collection." May 2019. https://www2.ed.gov/about/offices/list/ocr/docs/school-climate-and-safety.pdf.

Villarosa, Linda. "Why America's Black Mothers and Babies Are in a Life-or-Death Crisis." *New York Times Magazine*, April 11, 2018. https://www.nytimes.com/2018/04/11/magazine/black-mothers-babies-death-maternal-mortality.html.

Weeks, Virginia. "Fairness in the Exceptions: Trusting Juries on Matters of Race." *Michigan Journal of Race and Law* 23 (2018) 189–210. https://repository.law.umich.edu/cgi/viewcontent.cgi?article=1282&context=mjrl.

Weir, Kirsten. "Inequality at school: What's Behind the Racial Disparity in Our Education System?" *Monitor on Psychology* 47:10 (November 2016). https://www.apa.org/monitor/2016/11/cover-inequality-school.

West, Cornel. *Race Matters*. New York: Vintage, 2001.

Bibliography

Williams, Timothy. "Study Supports Suspicion That Police Are More Likely to Use Force on Blacks." *New York Times*, July 7, 2016. https://www.nytimes.com/2016/07/08/us/study-supports-suspicion-that-police-use-of-force-is-more-likely-for-blacks.html.

Wise, Tim. *White Like Me: Reflections on Race from a Privileged Son*. Brooklyn: Soft Skull, 2005.

Workneh, Lilly. "Two Trailblazers on Growing Up Black and Female in the North and South." *HuffPost*, September 26, 2017. https://www.huffpost.com/entry/two-black-trailblazing-women-on-overcoming-racial-barriers-to-achieve-success_n_59c52d76e4b06ddf45f77a6c.

Yancy, George. *Backlash: What Happens When We Talk Honestly about Racism in America*. Lanham, MD: Rowman & Littlefield, 2018.

———. *Black Bodies, White Gazes: The Continuing Significance of Race in America*. 2nd ed. Lanham, MD: Rowman and Littlefield, 2017.

———. *Look, a White!: Philosophical Essays on Whiteness*. Philadelphia: Temple University Press, 2012.

"Your Stories of Racism." *The Atlantic*, July 13, 2015. https://www.theatlantic.com/national/archive/2015/07/your-stories-of-racism/398117/.

www.ingramcontent.com/pod-product-compliance
Lightning Source LLC
Chambersburg PA
CBHW062044220426
43662CB00010B/1652